D1626291

031724

Elements & Total Concept of

URBAN
LANDSCAPE
DESIGN

日本のランドスケープの将来

ガレット・エクボ

　歴史的にみて，日本のランドスケープは恐らく世界の中で最も保存と管理が行き届いている例である。古都，田園，農地，けわしい山，海岸，岩石，洞窟，崖，河川，湖沼，などすべて日本の文化遺産にとって不可欠の要素になっている。毎年，何千もの人々が先人によってもたらされた自然的文化的な遺産を見聞しようとして各地を訪れている。

　庭園，住居，神社仏閣，皇居，城郭など日本古来の建築やランドスケープのデザインは日本の自然がもたらした人間の営みの大きな流れを，優雅にかつ洗練された形で表現してきた。このような日本の人間と自然は，世界の中でも歴史的にも文化的にも貴重かつ重要な作品であり，西洋のそれよりさらに整合性があり，洗練されている。

　ペリーの来航と明治維新によって，政治，経済，文化などが西洋から急激に移入され，都市における技術や経済の発展はほぼ西洋と同じようになったが，細かいところには日本独特のものが残されている。日本の公園は，18世紀のヨーロッパの公園に似たものが多い。（金沢の面積20エーカーに及ぶ大きく古い公園のように，真の都市公園として機能しているものもあるが……。）日本の文化は世界で最も永続性があると思われるが，欧米からの全世界的な商業主義的文化の影響を多大に受けてしまった。ニューヨークと東京，ロスアンゼルスと大阪などは今日的世界的な都市の様相を帯びている。

　西洋では，公園や庭などの細部のデザインは人間と自然を別個のものとして切り離して設計する伝統があった。地中海，ヨーロッパ，アメリカなど古典的でルネッサンス調のほとんどのデザインは，人工的に自然界の幾何学紋様を再編成する表現を行ってきた。18世紀の英国では，自然のすべては庭園であると意識してデザインした成功例があったが，現在の西洋はフォーマルとインフォーマルの両方の伝統的スタイルをもっており，お互いを一緒に決して受け入れようとはしない。われわれ西洋人はこれらの二つの分裂が融合できるとは決して考えていない。

　一方，日本や中国ではこのような分裂対比がまったく存在しない。仏教も神道も人と自然も一体であり，縫い目のない織物のように織りなされているという思想があるからであろうか。これらのことは哲学的，宗教的な問題であるが結果としての作品に明白に現れている。すなわち東洋は西洋よりも，もっと自由に自然と人間とを融合させて設計しているのである。

　今世紀になって，西洋のランドスケープ・アーキテクトは，自然のままの土地や岩石，水，植物などの形態を生かして，従来の概念に縛られない，左右対称ではない幾何学的相互関係を作りはじめてきた。しかし，いまだ十分とはいえずその道程は遠いように思われる。

　日本は西洋の現代のデザイナーがいまだに求め続けている質的な最終目標を成就するために，自らの伝統的な形態を応用して，現代のデザイン・ボキャブラリーをさらに発展させ，作り上げていく可能性に満ちている。空間の構成や，自然の形態と人間が作った形態と材質の間の詳細な相互関係，ビルの形態や周辺の景観の認識，すなわち建物の形態やまわりの空間へのこまやかな配慮，材料の可能性や潜在能力，人々の要求や反応，それぞれの土地の特質などの認識をすること，これらのすべてにその解答が用意されている。

（都田　徹・訳）

FUTURE JAPANESE LANDSCAPE

Garrett Eckbo

The Japanese historical landscape is probably one of the best preserved and most carefully maintained in the world. Old central cities, rural villages, farm lands and wild mountains, seashores and beaches, rocks, caves, and cliffs, rivers and lakes, are all seen as integral elements in the Japanese cultural heritage. Every year thousands go on pilgrimage to experience this national wealth provided by nature with close participation by the people.

Japanese classical architecture and landscape design, in gardens, houses, temples, shrines, palaces, and castles, have for 2000 years given exquisite refined expression to this great history of human life with the nature of the Japanese islands. All together they are one of the most important historical cultural artifacts of the world, more consistently and coherently refined than anything in the West.

Since Admiral Perry and the Meiji period the West has made increasingly forceful economic, political, and cultural incursions into Japan. Technical and business developments in the central cities are increasingly similar in general, although specifically Japanese in detail. Most parks in Japanese cities have the aspect of 18th century European parks (although in Kanazawa there is a great old 20-acre garden which serves as an authentic urban park). Even though Japanese culture is not only the richest but probably the most durable in the world, cosmopolitan commercial culture from Europe and America have had a tremendous impact on it. New York and Tokyo, Los Angeles and Osaka, are the world cities of tomorrow today.

In terms of the detailed design of buildings, parks, and gardens, the West has a tradition which carefully separates man from nature. Classical and Renaissance design throughout the Mediterranean, Europe, and America has expressed the geometric organization of nature by man. In the 18th century in England there was a stroke of conscience which discovered that all nature was a garden. Now the West has two traditions, formal and informal, but has never tried to put them together into one. We cannot seem to heal the split.

In Japan, and China, such a split has never existed. In Buddhist and Shinto thought man and nature are one world, one seamless web. While these are matters of philosophy and religion, the physical result is clear. The forms of nature and of human design seem to mix more freely in the Orient than they do in the Occident.

In this century, in the West, the works of modern or contemporary landscape architects have begun to bridge the gap, with irregular and asymmetrical geometry interlocking with natural ground, rock, water, and plant forms. But this has a long way to go. Japan has the potential for developing a modern design vocabulary, based on expansion and variations from its traditional forms, that will achieve qualitative goals for which western modern designers are still seeking. Combinations of the open center, detailed interaction between natural and man-made forms and materials, recognition of building forms and of surrounding landscapes; intensive attention to the form and sequence of space, the properties and potentialities of materials, and the needs and responses of people, all recognizing the special qualities of each site and its locality, will provide the answers.

目次

Contents

1. 庭のデザインからランドスケープのデザインに

戦後40年，日本はその先端技術の開発と正比例し，目覚ましい経済成長を遂げた。最近では技術（便利さ）から豊かさに，ハードからソフトへと社会の価値観も変化し，真の豊かさとは何か？潤いとは何か？余裕とは何か？など生活の利便性から精神の問題へと価値観も変化しつつある。

国際化と技術革新の谷間にあって，日本の造園界もようやく伝統的な庭のデザインの時代からランドスケープ・デザインの時代へと入りつつあるように思われる。

住宅に対応する庭のスケールから，国土とランドスケープ（自然）の問題へ，そしてこれらは自然と開発，都市と自然，保存と開発などの問題といったスケールに変化してきている。社会の国際化にともなう人々のグローバルな動きによって，もはや専門家集団のみのデザインや機能優先のデザインにとどまらず，生態系を考えたデザインや住民参加のデザインの問題へと変化を来している。

2. ランドスケープ・デザイン・エレメントへの問題提起

人間のライフスタイルの変化に伴って，人間の生活環境や社会も次第に変化を来しており，現在もっとも必要とされていることとして地球上の人間相互の調和の問題，動物と人間の調和の問題，植物と人間の調和の問題，また動物と植物の調和の問題などが上げられる。その解決の糸口をランドスケープ・デザインに求めるとするならば，それら相互間の生態系を大切にするアプローチであったり，使い手側の参加も含めたデザインワークだとか，色々な試みがなされなければならない。

しかしもっとも大切なことは，これまでに見られるような自然と都市，または自然と開発といった二者択一の論理よりも共存共栄，ともに相和する平和と調和の論理の大切さである。

ランドスケープ・デザイン界においてもこうした概念をベースにしてようやく人間を含めた使う側（ユーザー）とユーザーの生活全体，その場所を真に使いたくなるような使い手に喜ばれ，その場が生きる空間の論理を中心としたアプローチに目が向けられるのが至当であろう。

このアプローチにとって大切な視点は，使い手も含めたその「場の情景」をまず考え，これらの情景をエレメントに分析し，このエレメントの組み合せにより景観を構成し，次第に練り上げていくことにより，そこにエレメントが使われる必然性としての風景が描写されていくことである。

これら一連のプロセスをわれわれはトータル・ランドスケープ・エレメントと呼び，この小冊子で何らかの問いかけを行ったつもりである。ランドスケープをエレメントを中心として捉えようとした試みは我が国で初めてである。

すでに完成している作品に対し写真による参加を求め，上記したコンセプトを何とか表現してみたいと願ったのであるが，応募側や使い手側に特にデザイン・エレメントを分析し余すところなく記録する視点があることは稀であり，狙い通りの記録写真が収録できたとは言いがたい。従って当初のコンセプトが十分表現できたとは言えない。今回の試みやデザイン・エレメントに対しての解釈に異論はあろうが，この本が一つの踏み台として将来へのステップとなりランドスケープ・デザインや環境デザインの発展に寄与できれば幸いである。

先に述べたプロセス・アプローチは今後のランドスケープの空間の中にヒトが生きる空間の連続性をつくり，様々なデザイン・エレメントがその時代性とともに人々の生活を象徴し，「生きる場」のアイデンティティを主張する答えをつくってくれるであろうと確信している。今回の試みがさらに発展展開され，すぐれたデザイン・エレメントによって21世紀へと架橋するさらに新らたな環境がデザインされ，それを可能とするエレメントがさらに出現することを願っている。

(T. M & M. N)

Total Landscape Design and Elements

1. ## From garden design to landscape design
   ## (the meaning of Total Landscape Design)

   Forty years have passed since the disaster of war, and with proper technological development Japan has seen tremendous growth. Recently society's values have changed, though, and technology wealth (convenience) is coming into question. Values are changing from 'hard' to 'soft'. Questions like 'what is the value of such wealth?' and 'what is gained' are being asked. As life becomes easier, issues of the spirit are becoming the rule.

   Against this backdrop, in a country on the brink of internationalization and technological revolution, the age of traditional Japanese garden design is entering the new age of landscape design.

   From house gardens to the civil landscaping projects, including development of the natural environment and the urban-nature environment, conservation and related issues are becoming problems of major scale. With the internationalization of society has come global movement of people, and added to the state-of-the-art design by major specialists groups, and new environmental design and 'citizen-assisted' design concepts, more change is forthcoming.

2. ## The landscape design scene

   Accompanying the process of human lifestyle evolution, the living environment develops, and needs are observed. The modern needs no being recognized are equilibrium between man and the planet, between man and animal, man and plants, and plants and animals. These are the primary issues of the day. In an effort to bring about successful approaches to these problems, those who work at creating man's living environment are joining hands and attempting various new design solutions.

   But more than the previously important theories of city vs. nature, and development of the natural region, the concept of coexistence and prosperity—the theory peaceful equilibrium—is being emphasized as most important. Now, in the landscape design world, eyes are being turned toward the concept of a living environment where the user lives happily, in a true 'living' space, which can bring out his desire to be there and use it. This is the ideal now being adopted.

   What is important in this approach is, first, to think of the user as part of the landscape, and to analyse different elements of this landscape so that they can be composed in a sketch.

   This is the process called 'total landscape approach' and it is the purport of this book to reveal this process. Records of both first efforts and completed, photographed designs, were to be published in this volume, but contributors could offer few fully realized 'analyses', so this book must stand as a stepping stone to a more complete, future edition.

   The aforementioned 'process approach' should do much to help landscape to unify the total design of space, to symbolize human life and instill environmental identity. As an affirmation of this movement the present volume exhibits expectations of the future developments.

Elements & Total Concept of

URBAN LANDSCAPE DESIGN

ISBN 4-7661-0475-7
Manufactured in Japan
First Edition April 1988
Graphic-sha Publishing Co., Ltd.
1-9-12 Kudankita Chiyoda-ku
Tokyo 102 Japan

Elements & Total Concept of

URBAN LANDSCAPE DESIGN

凡 例

a. 作品名
b. 所在地
c. クライアント
d. ディレクター，設計監修
e. インダストリアルデザイナー，エンジニア，コーディネーター，設計，設計協力，
　　造形デザイナー，彫刻家，デザイナー，デザイン計画，プロダクトマネージャー，
　　モニュメント作家，メーカー
f. 施工者
g. 撮影者，写真提供
h. コメント
i. 主な使用材料
j. 応募代表者

Caption Information

a. Project name
b. Location
c. Client
d. Director, etc.
e. Industrial designer, Engineer, Planning, Drafting, Technical
　　Design, Sculpting, Designer, Management, Monument,
　　Manufacturer etc.
f. Coordinating
g. Photographer
h. Comments
i. Materials
j. Representatives/Contributors

1.開港広場 歴史を刻むモニュメント広場

　1854年、わが国は日米親善条約をこの広場の近くで締結、1858年には日米修好条約が結ばれ、1859年横浜港は世界に向けて華々しく開港した。それを記念して設置されたのがこの広場である。

　ここは旧英国領事館(現開港資料館)、旧英一番館跡であるシルクセンター、海岸教会などが建っている由緒ある場所であり、西洋文明の波がひた寄せていた。北には世界的に有名な大桟橋がある。また山下公園への導入部になっていて、いわば横浜の「へそ」ともいうべき場所であるが、以前は変則的な交差点となっていた。車の流れをスムーズにすると同時に開港を記念するにふさわしい広場として整備することになり、当時建設省が打ち出した広場公園の横浜における第1号の誕生であった。

設計に当たって

　文明開化の地を永久に記念する「ほとばしる文明」をテーマとした噴水は「開港の泉」と称し、まわりのピンコロは西欧文明が押し寄せる波を表現している。金峰石のピンコロと白大理石のピンコロを特注し白線を描き波のうねりと共に文明の息吹きを表わした。

　噴水の足元部分に「じゃぶじゃぶ池」を設けた。設計者の願いは子供たちが夏の暑い日にズボンをまくり上げじゃぶじゃぶ遊んでくれたり、裸になって水と戯れてくれる光景であり、それを想像しながら図面を描いた。もちろん、大人にも楽しんでもらえるに違いない。そう確信してデザインした。安全には十分注意した。もっとも深いところで、水深15センチ、顔を横にして押しつけない限りまず安全である。

　噴水の部分にピットがある。その蓋にも一味違った趣向を凝らしたかった。ペリーがその昔日本に来航した船の羅針盤を形に採りたかった。横須賀の米海軍やワシントンにも問い合わせたが不明であった。やむなく羅針盤の専門書にその原形を求め、1850年代の代表的な形を忠実に再現するデザインを試みた。

　噴水を取り囲むステンレス鏡面のモニュメントは、現代文明を映し出す鏡である。周辺の建物や移り変わる状況を映し出している。12個設置し「時の流れ」をイメージしている。鏡面はまわりの景色に溶け込んで不思議な効果を生み出している。

　ロジェ・カイヨワ(Roger Caillois・仏の哲学者)は遊びには「偶然」「眩暈」「競争」「模擬」の四つの要素があると説いている。このうち「偶然」と「眩暈」につながる効果を出したかったのである。

　このミラーの足元に集光型のランプを埋め込み12条の光が放たれる。訪れる人影が近づくと光がゆらゆら揺らめき面白い効果を上げている。

　ステンレスの鏡面ミラーの反射によってドライバーを幻惑させてはならない。不測の事故に備えて原寸大の模型を持ち込み危険が無いことを確認した。

　横浜の国際親善都市および横浜と提携している港などが10ケ所ある。それらの都市と提携している港の市章や紋章をブロンズにレリーフして埋め込んでいる。

　工事中に発見された明治時代の見事なマンホールは上からのぞき込めるようにガラスで蓋をし丁重に保存、先人への敬意を表した。

　環境デザインに対する一般の理解が今日ほど無かった当時としては、歴史的に有意義な地区の広場づくりに参加でき、綿密な調査に基づいた設計と、新しい試みが許されたことを感謝している。横浜は世界の「よこはま」として再びよみがえろうとしている。

　われわれの仕事が、その先駆的役割をいささかでも果たしているとすれば、望外の幸せである。

(高橋志保彦)

a. 開港広場
b. 神奈川県横浜市
c. 横浜市都市計画局、緑政局、下水道局、道路局
d. 高橋志保彦
e. 高橋志保彦、松本裕
f. 横浜植木㈱
g. 北原美子(北井スタジオ)、高橋志保彦
j. 高橋志保彦建築設計事務所

a. A SQUARE TO COMMEMORATE HISTORY
b. Yokohama-shi, Kanagawa
c. The City of Yokohama Urban Plannig Bureau, Green Environment Administration Bureau, Sewerage System Bureau, Road & Highway Bureau
d. Shiohiko Takahashi
e. Shiohiko Takahashi, Yu Matsumoto
f. Yokohama Ueki Co., Ltd.
g. Yoshiko Kitahara (Kitai Studio), Shiohiko Takaha- shi
j. Shiohiko Takahashi, SHIOHIKO TAKAHASHI ARCHITECTS & ASSOCIATE.

a. 横浜港を臨む広場全景
a. FULL VIEW OF YOKOHAMA HARBOR

a. 噴水「開港の泉」とモニュメント
i. ステンレス鏡面仕上げ

a. THE "HARBOR SPRING" FOUNTAIN AND
MONUMENT

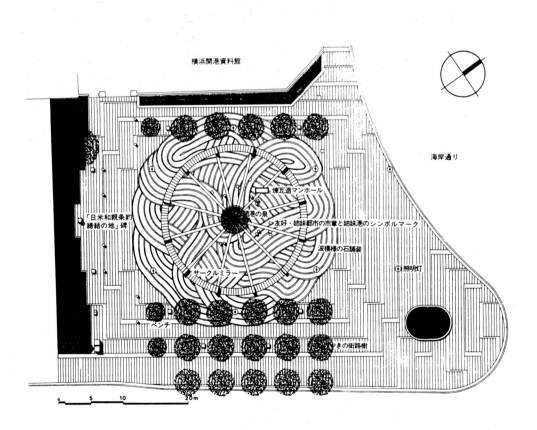

横浜開港資料館

海岸通り

煉瓦造マンホール
開港の泉
友好・姉妹都市の市章と姉妹港のシンボルマーク
波模様の石舗装
「日米和親条約締結の地」碑
サークルミラー
照明灯
ベンチ
けやきの街路樹

0　5　10　20m

a. スツール
a. STOOL

g. 高橋志保彦
g. Shiohiko Takahashi

g. 高橋志保彦
g. Shiohiko Takahashi

a. 車止とベンチ　　　　a. WHEL BLOCK BENCH
i. ステンレス／ヒノキ　i. Cypress and stainless steel

VANCOUVER CANADA
バンクーバー　カナダ
7676.1㎞　44°19'14"

OAKLAND U.S.A
オークランド　アメリカ
8909.7㎞　54°12'2"

SAN DIEGO U.S.A
サンディエゴ　アメリカ
8999.7㎞　56°0'8"

LYON FRANCE
リヨン　フランス
9909.9㎞　330°19'30"

CONSTANTA ROMANIA
コンスタンツァ　ルーマニア
8759.9㎞　316°51'23"

a. 姉妹都市と姉妹港のレリーフ
h. 左の数字は横浜からの距離、右側の数字は時計回りによる角度によって方位をあらわす。

a. Relief for Sister Cities and Sister Ports.
h. The lefthand figure represents the distance from Yokohama, while the righthand number shows the direction via the movement of the clockhand.

PORT OF MELBOURNE
メルボルン　オーストラリア
8164.4㎞　175°37'12"

MANILA PHILIPPINES
マニラ　フィリピン
2972㎞　223°25'8"

BOMBAY INDIA
ボンベイ　インド
6732.2㎞　266°51'36"

SHANGHAI CHINA
シャンハイ　中国
1745.1㎞　259°35'18"

ODESSA U.S.S.R
オデッサ　ソビエト
8479.2㎞　317°54'7"

A Square to Commemorate History

In 1854, near this square, the Japanese-American Goodwill Treaty was signed, followed in 1858 by the signing of the Japanese-American Friendship Treaty. In 1859 the port of Yokohama was opened to the world with great pomp. This square stands in commemoration these events.

Found about this historical place are such structures as the old English consulate, the ruins of the English First Residence Silk Centre, and the Coast Church. The new waves of western culture first washed ashore here. To the north is the world famous Sambashi Bridge. In the direction of the entrace to Yamashita Koen is so called 'umbilicus' of Yokohama, once an irregular intersection that the city construction department reconstructed to control traffic smoothly and at the same time commemorate the opening of Yokohama port. It marked a first birthday for Yokohama.

On Planning

As an eternal commemoration of the world's 'bursting' civilization the fountain here is called the 'Port Spring'. The stones which surround it recall the waves of western culture approaching Japan. The white and gold stones are concentrated to represent the crests of the waves and the lifebreath of culture.

There is a 'cavorting' basin around the base of the fountain, designed by the planner to offer children a place to cool off on hot summer days. Adults as well are welcome to roll up their pants and dip their feet. The depth of the water is only fifteen centimeters at most, reflecting the planner's concern for safety.

On the fountain there is also what looks to be a lid, modeled after the compass which Perry had when he arrived in Yokohama. Efforts to complete the design involved contacts with the Yokosuka U. S. Naval contingent and Washington. Finally a book on compasses was acquired, and true-to-life model of the period's compass was achieved.

The stainless steel mirror which surrounds the fountain reflects modern civilization and the surrounding environment. The twelve-part asssembly suggests the flow of time and a strange, colorful image of the world around it.

The French philosopher Roger Caillois explained that play has four different aspects, coincidence, dizziness, competition and imitation. Of these the ideas of coincidence and dizziness apply here.

At the base of this mirror twelve lamps are embedded, emitting twelve stripes of light. The shadows of visitors interact with these lights in various ways as they approach, creating interesting results.

In order that drivers not be blinded by the reflections of the stainless mirror, a model was moved in and the safety of the model established.

Yokohama's ten international friendship cities and ports of the world have their crests and insignias embedded in bronze here.

A Meiji-period manhole which was unearthed during construction has been preserved under glass for posterity's sake, and place where all can clearly view it.

We have to be thankful for the efforts made at that time, when mach less thought was generally given to the environment. New ideas were attempted, and plans carefully drawn up and executed. Yokohama became a city of the world, and we are now looking to reestablish it as such.

We will be proud if our work can claim as much excellence as this farsighted effort of long ago. (Shiohiko Takahashi)

2.別府市庁舎広場

追憶と希望，心に描くキャンバス

市庁舎の広場は市役所を訪れる市民にとっても，外来のお客様にとっても観光都市別府のオフィシャルな玄関としてみなさんを温かく迎える顔になっていることが望ましい，と考えた。

同時にこの広場は地域の自然，歴史，文化を表現し21世紀への時代を刻みこんでいく，あるいは未来を自由に描いていく「白いキャンバス」としての役割を持たせたかった。　市の行政を司る行政棟の軸線は別府湾に一直線に伸びている。この軸から出る

エネルギーを「波型」の地模様で受け，隣接の別府公園に拡散させるデザインである。そのモチーフは「別府湾に打ち寄せるさざ波」であり階段がその具体化である。その奥にある滝と共に，全体のデザインに対するエレメントとして砂浜，海面，高波として見ていただければ幸いである。

その他，広場のデザインエレメントの絡み合いで生き生きとした表情を持つ空間を演出してみた。

・単純な曲線を描く落水

・ハードな舗装とソフトな樹木

・階段のリズムと樹木の静寂

・過ぎ行く人とたたずむ人

時には饒舌であり，あるときは寡黙である。相反する性格を表すこの広場は，ここで働く人にとっても，訪れる人にとっても心の中に忍び込み愛され明日を生きる喜びを与え続け，何かを描き続ける「追憶と希望のキャンバス」として存在し続けて欲しい。

（戸田芳樹）

a. 別府市庁舎広場
b. 大分県別府市
c. 別府市
d. 戸田芳樹
e. ㈱戸田芳樹＋風景計画，地福由紀，島川清史，奈木政幸
f. 大成・梅林・三光建設工事共同企業体
g. 地福由紀
j. ㈱戸田芳樹＋風景計画

a. BEPPU MUNICIPAL OFFICE SQUARE
b. Beppu-shi, Ohita
c. Beppu City
d. Yoshiki Toda
e. Toda Yoshiki & Fukei Keikaku Associates, Yuki Jifuku, Kiyoshi Simakawa, Masayuki Nagi
f. Taisei, Umebayashi, Sanko Construction Works J. V.
g. Yuki Jifuku
j. Toda Yoshiki & Fukei Keikaku Associates

a. 白糸の滝　a. The Shiraito Fall

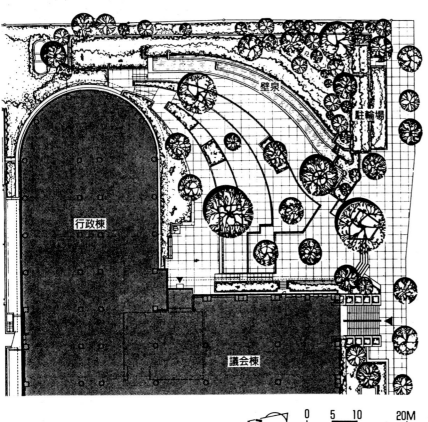

壁泉

駐輪場

行政棟

議会棟

0　5　10　　20M

a. 植栽とペーブメント
h. 打ち寄せる波を表現
a. Planting and Pavement
h. It expresses the wash of waves

a. 植栽とペーブメント
h. 打ち寄せる波を表現

a. ベンチ	a. BENCH
e. 奈木政幸	e. Masayuki Nagi
h. 広場のスケールと植栽の景観にマッチするよう、重厚なイメージとして設計した。	h. Designed imposingly to fit the square and pavement

a. 水飲み	a. DRINKIG FOUNTAIN
e. 奈木政幸	e. Masayuki Nagi
h. ファニチュアとしての機能と庁舎の外観を象徴的に取り入れてデザインした。	h. Designed for use as furniture and symbolized the exterior of the building.

Beppu City Office Square

A canvas for memories and hopes

The Beppu city office was designed to offer a warm face and official welcome to local people and visitors to Beppu alike.

At the same time the square was intended to evoke the natural setting and historical backdrop of the locale in an expression of movement into the twenty-first century. A 'white canvas', open to the future, is harbored in the design of the square.

The municipal buildings form the axis of the city, in a line which extends down to the sea. The energy which emanates from this line spreads like ripples over the nearby land, which includes the city park. This 'emanating' is part of the design, and the motif of 'waves washing ashore' is expressed concretely by the steps. Beyond steps there is a waterfall. The sand, high waves and sea are the overall elements of this design.

The elements of this design work together to create attractive, living space.

／The simple, bending lines of falling water
／Hard pavement and soft trees
／Rhythmic steps and solemn arbour
／Passing people and motionless people

At times talkative, the scene may later become reticent. This square exhibits such a varied personality, in a way that the people who work here and the people who visit hear a bright future calling. A desire to live on and to paint a canvas of hope is instilled in the viewers heart.

(Yoshiki Toda)

3.新田緑道　　住民も参加した新しい街づくり

　新田緑道は，生産と生活が共存している準工業地域の特色を反映した緑道＝インダストリアル・コミュニティ・モール（人と工場との全く新しい出会いの道）として設計され，その整備が進められています。

　昔はさまざまな街の中に工場があったり，職人さんの姿が見受けられたりして，働くことの意義や作られている物の大切さなどを学びとっていました。

　今では多くの工場や町工場が臨海地域や工業団地に移っていき，この新田のような準工業地域こそ物を生産する現場が見られる数少ない場所といえます。

　緑道の設計にあたって，ここに住む人たちや工場で働く人たちが心からくつろげ，ふれあえる緑豊かな地域環境整備の核とすると共に，地域の人々が

町の誇りとして他の町の人々に自慢できるように，この地域の特色を生かしてデザインの中に工業の色合いを取り入れました。

　具体的には，チェーンの路，歯車の路，プレートの路など，各ブロックを機械の構成部分をテーマとして形づくり，ファニュチュア類も，パイプのモニュメントやボルト型車止，エンジン遊具，歯車やプーリーなどを組み込んだパーゴラなどを設置し，昔のせせらぎを復活させた流れにはパイプのシャワーなどを設けました。また，地元の工場で長い間使われ愛着を持たれてきた機械をモニュメントにしたり，スクラップを利用して組み立てた複合機械モニュメントを計画し雰囲気づくりをしています。

　更に，この緑道の整備を進めていく上での特徴と

して，住民参加の方式を取り入れたことが上げられます。緑道が住民と工場で働く人たちに愛され親しまれいくためには，その計画施工段階からいっしょに作りあげるという認識が不可欠です。園路や流れの中に埋め込まれた手作りの平板は，地域の人々が自らの手でタイルや貝殻を埋め込んでつくったものです。

　ふれあい花壇は老人会の手でいつも手入れされ花いっぱい。せせらぎの清掃も住民の手で行われています。地域に根ざしたデザインの緑道が人々の手で大切に育てられていますが，今後は緑道を核として周辺工場のファサードの美化や緑化など街全体の環境整備へ反映させていくことが望まれます。

（高野文彦）

a. 新田緑道
b. 神奈川県横浜市
c. 横浜市
d. 高野文彦
f. 相武造園土木㈱
g. 北原美子（北井スタジオ）　高野ランドスケーププランニング㈱
j. 高野ランドスケーププランニング㈱

a. NITTA INDUSTRIAL COMMUNITY MALL
b. Kohoku-ku, Yokohama
c. Yokohama City
d. Fumiaki Takano
f. Sobu Zoen Doboku Co., Ltd.
g. Yoshiko Kitahara (Kitai Studio), Takano Landscape Planning Co., Ltd.
j. TAKANO LANDSCAPE PLANNING Co., Ltd.

チェーンの路　A Chain Path

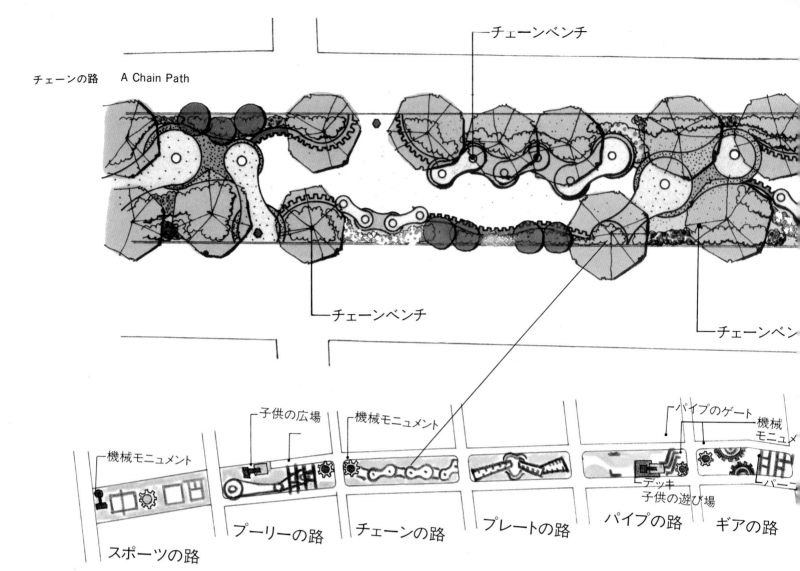

チェーンベンチ

チェーンベンチ

チェーンベン

機械モニュメント

子供の広場

機械モニュメント

パイプのゲート

機械モニュメ

デッキ
子供の遊び場

パイ

スポーツの路　プーリーの路　チェーンの路　プレートの路　パイプの路　ギアの路

新田緑道　　　A Path through Verdure

花の路　　　A Path through Blossom

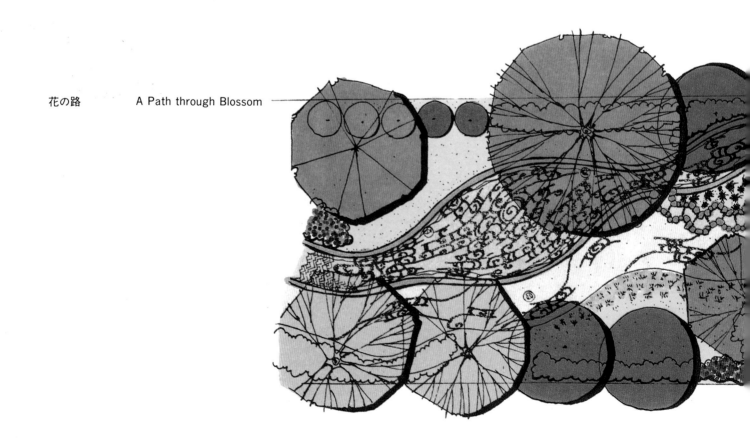

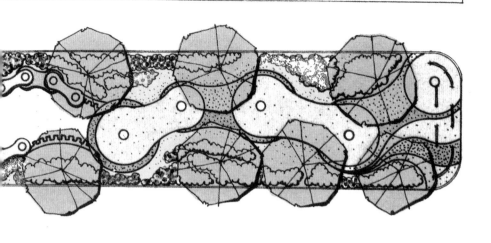

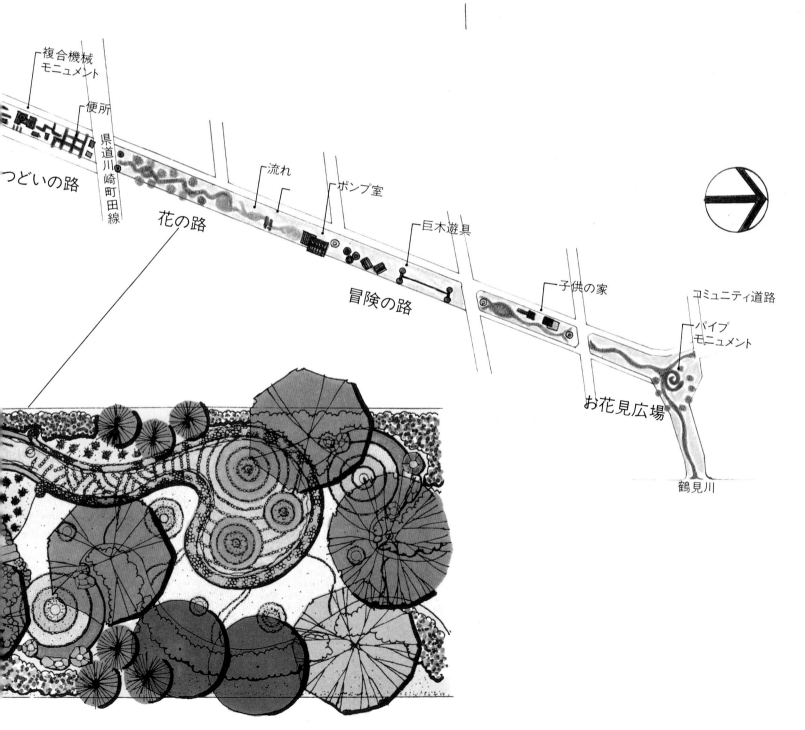

複合機械
モニュメント

便所

県道川崎町田線

つどいの路

花の路

流れ

ポンプ室

巨木遊具

冒険の路

子供の家

コミュニティ道路

パイプ
モニュメント

お花見広場

鶴見川

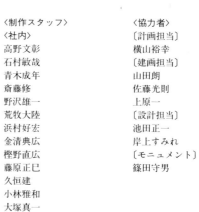

〈制作スタッフ〉　　　〈協力者〉
〈社内〉　　　　　　　〔計画担当〕
高野文彰　　　　　　　横山裕幸
石村敏哉　　　　　　　〔建画担当〕
青木成年　　　　　　　山田朗
斎藤修　　　　　　　　佐藤光則
野沢雄一　　　　　　　上原一
荒牧大陸　　　　　　　〔設計担当〕
浜村好宏　　　　　　　池田正一
金清典広　　　　　　　岸上すみれ
樫野直広　　　　　　　〔モニュメント〕
藤原正巳　　　　　　　篠田守男
久恒建
小林雅和
大塚真一

a. 流れ
h. 昔あった流れを再現し，途中に水車や噴水を設け
　子供たちが遊べる環境となるようデザインした。
a. Stream
h. It is reproduced the same form as it was, and
　provided a water wheel and a fountain for children
　to play.

(STAFF)
Fumiaki Takano
Toshiya Ishimura
Shigetoshi Aoki
Osamu Saito
Yuichi Nozawa
Dairiku Aramaki
Yoshihiro Hamamura
Norihiro Kanekiyo
Naohiro Kashino
Masami Fujiwara
Ken Hisatsune
Masakazu Kobayashi
Shinichi Otsuka

(Cooperation)
〈Planning〉
Hiroyuki Yokoyama
〈Architects〉
Akira Yamada
Mitsunori Sato
Hajime Uehara
〈Design〉
Shoichi Ikeda
Sumire Kishigami
〈Monument〉
Morio Shinoda

a. モニュメント
h. 工場で使用されていた器械
a. Monument
h. A machine used in a factory

a. モニュメント
h. 工場で使われていた機械に手を加えて保存した。
a. Monument
h. A machine used in a factory is touched up and
 preserved.

g. 高野ランドスケープ
g. TAKANO LANDSCAPE

g. 高野ランドスケープ
g. TAKANO LANDSCAPE

a. ペーブパターン
h. 住民も参加して制作された。
a. PAVEMENT PATTERN
h. Produced by the assistance of the inhabitants.

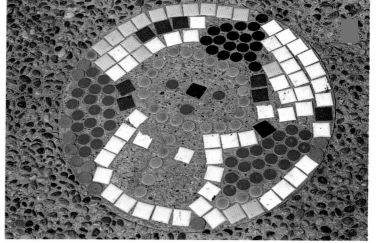

a. 入口
h. 町工場の公園にふさわしいデザインとした。
a. Entrance
h. It is designed suitable for a park of a small factory.

a. 車止
h. ボルトを形どったデザイン。
a. Car stop
h. It is designed in the shape of a bolt.

Mall Elements

Rebuilding with the people

Nitta Green Mall represents "birth" and "activity", industry and the public living together hand in an industrial area. The Green Mall is an industrial community's mall, a completely new realization of man and industry in a common environment.

In the past, factories existed in the towns. Workers were seen and their work was before everyone's eyes. The importance of the product and its maker was understood from direct experience.

Now, when so much industry is being moved to coastal areas and 'technopolis' developments, the producing local industry is a phenomenon not frequently seen.

The Nitta Green Mall development was planned to give the local residents and factory workers a pleasant environment, and something they might be proud of. The local flavor was brought out and the factory influence well considered in the planning.

Specifically, the mall has a chain path, cogwheel path and plate path, which conform to the themes of each separate block. Street furniture as well is made of pipe, and there are pipe monuments, curbs and meters made of factory bolts,

engines to play on and pergola made of cogwheel cars, etc. The brook which once flowed has been revived, flowing through pipes and showers. Machines which were used for many years at the factory, and scrap material, have been molded into different monuments, adding to the atmosphere.

But what is being emphasized most about the Green Mall project is the participation of the local citizenry. In order that the mall be popular with the people and workers, the planning of the project has involved their opinions at every stare. The tilework along the way is crafted by the people themselves, who can feel they have really had a hand in the creation of the park.

The flower stand is under the care of the senior citizens association, who see to it that flowers are always fresh. The cleaning of the stream is also the work of the people. The value of the cooperation of the citizens is fully appreciated in the Green Mall project. In the future it is hoped that the project will beget further beautification work on the factory fascade, which would add a central element to the theme of the project.

(Fumihiko Takano)

4.パークシティ・新川崎

関係者の英知が創造した住いと環境

ランドスケープ・デザインにおいて，集合住宅のデザインはどちらかといえば表面的には地味な仕事である。人々が住まい，活動し，憩う毎日の日常性の中に，ランドスケープデザインの展開をすることは他の対象に比べて難しい面をもっており，それだけにやり甲斐のある問題でもある。それは集合住宅としての街の中に人々が生活を営んでいく街づくりが，最終的なテーマとなるだけに他の対象よりも難しい困難な問題を一つ一つ克服していかねばならないからである。

パークシティ新川崎の場合，全体約6haの中央部にセントラルアベニューという流れを伴った緑道を中心として，東西3ブロックづつ計6つのブロックがある。東ブロックの南端はデベロッパーによる提供小学校となり，従って，この街は五街区よりなる1800戸，6000人の街が形成されている。このスケールで，人々が生き生きとした生活を送る"街"を

デザインするためにわれわれは数々の工夫を行っている。

中央部の流れは近くを流れる多摩川を象徴しており，これは南端のギャラリー広場のひょうたん池の噴水から涌き出した水が一度地下に潜り，滝となって流れ始め，橋や飛石をぬって，岩間に吸い込まれ，ここで地下に浸透した水が鯨の潮吹きを思わせるエンド部分のショッピングアリーナで再び噴水となる風景を演出した。

私達は上記のストーリーに達するまでに，デベロッパーの企画室，広告代理店，施工会社の設計部，施工者，そして各種モニュメントのデザイナー達と何回となく，ミーティングを行った。徹底した討論の結果，シークェンス（連続感）の要として流れを設定し，これに伴うエレメントの展開は流れ沿いのペーブメントに，縁石に，立ち上がりに，そして最終的にはここで生活を営む人たちがその生活空間に

対して充実感を味合うことが出来るように，方向を定めていった。いわば関係者一同の英知の結集によって新しい"街"が創造されていったと言ってもよかろう。

ポイント，ポイントに配したランドマークとしてのモニュメントやエレメントは，それぞれの場において，アイデンティテイを主張しており，これらが集合住宅としての"街"に根付くことで全体としての空間の調和と一貫した連続性が表現されている。

エレメントの展開は水→ペーブメント→縁石→立ち上がり→モニュメント→飛石→橋にとどまらず，四季感を表現してくれる緑によって，場所・場所のアイデンティテイを更に強調することにより，パークシティでのテーマとしての，水と緑と空間と人間のトータルな統一感と一体感を表現出来たものと思っている。

（文責／中島幹夫，都田　徹）

a. パークシティ新川崎
b. 神奈川県川崎市
c. 三井不動産㈱
d. 三井不動産㈱・中島幹夫　上野卓二
e. 都田徹，緒方基秀，飯田清治
f. 鹿島建設㈱，三井建設㈱，㈱創研，関東コンクリート
g. 北原美子(北井スタジオ)，都田徹
j. 中島幹夫

a. PARK CITY SHIN-KAWASAKI
b. Kawasaki-shi, Kanagawa
c. Mitsui Real Estate Development
d. Mitsui Real Estate Development, Mikio Nakajima　Takuji Ueno
e. Tooru Miyakoda, Motohide Ogata, Seiji Iida
f. KAJIMA Corporation, Mitsui-Kensetsu, SOUKEN Co., Ltd., Kanto Concreet
g. Yoshiko Kitahara (Kitai Studio), Tooru Miyakoda
j. Mikio Nakajima

a. 噴水彫刻
h. モニュメントであると同時に子供たちの遊び場にも
　なっている。
a. SCULPTURE OF A FOUTAIN
h. The monument can also function as a place to play
　for children.

a. 噴水彫刻
h. モニュメントであると同時に子供たちの遊び場にも
　なっている。
a. SCULPTURE OF A FOUTAIN
h. The monument can also function as a place to play
　for children.

a. 流れ
h. 流れは住む人の心を和らげるとともに、遊び場にもなり防火用水路、落葉を集めて流す役割も果たしている。
a. STREAM
h. It eases inhabitant's mind and is used as play space and waterway for fire protection and leading fallen leaves away.

a. 流れ
h. 流れは住む人の心を和らげるとともに、遊び場にもなり防火用水路、落葉を集めて流す役割も果たしている。
a. STREAM
h. It eases inhabitant's mind and is used as play space and waterway for fire protection and leading fallen leaves away.

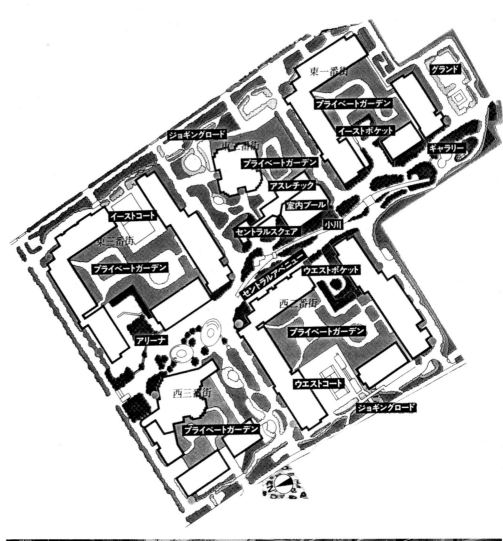

東一番街
プライベートガーデン
イーストポケット
グランド
ギャラリー
ジョギングロード
東一番街
プライベートガーデン
アスレチック
室内プール
イーストコート
セントラルスクェア
小川
東二番街
プライベートガーデン
セントラルアベニュー
ウエストポケット
西二番街
プライベートガーデン
アリーナ
ウエストコート
ジョギングロード
西三番街
プライベートガーデン

a. 噴水
h. モニュメントであるが子供たちは格好な遊び場にし
　　てくれる。
a. FOUNTAIN
h. The monument can also function as a place to play
　　for children.

a. ペーブパターン
h. それぞれの場所のアイデンティティを鮮明にするた
　め模様に変化をもたせた。
a. PAVEMENT PATTERN
h. It is designed variously to be identified with each
　place.

a. 屋上庭園
h. 駐車場内に自生していた大木を保存した。開口部
　は自然換気する。
a. ROOF GARDEN
h. A native big tree in the parking lot is preserved.
　The opening ventilates the room.

a. メタセコイアの林
a. METASEQUOIA WOOD

a. プラタナスの入口
a. ENTRANCE OF PLANES

a. シンボルツリー
a. A SYMBOLIC TREE

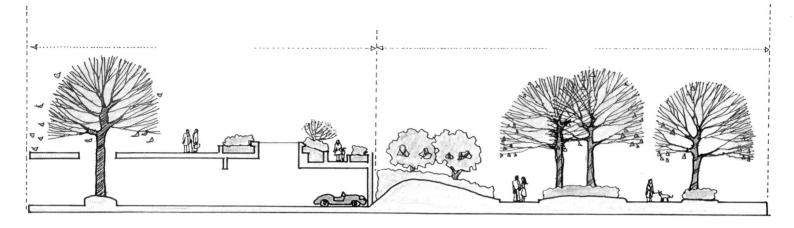

a. ポケット広場
a. POCKET SQUARE

a. 川辺の林(カツラ)
a. RIVERSIDE WOOD (KATSURA TREE)

a. 彫刻
e. 中島幹夫
a. Sculpture
e. Mikio Nakajima

Park City, Shin-Kawasaki

The apartment houses and surroundings created by wisdom of the persons concerned

As far as landscape design is usually concerned, the development of housing projects is rather sober work. But landscape design of areas where people spend every day of thier lives is also extremely difficult, and great care must be taken. Making the ideal 'a place where people can live and breathe' a final theme, presents a considerable challenge, but one that must be overcome.

In the case a Park City, Shin-Kawasaki, a green mall follows the flow of central avenue through the center of the downtown area. This area occupies three blocks to the east and west, for a total of six blocks. On the far edge of the eastern block will be an elementary school designed to the needs of an 1800 home, five ward town with a population of 6000. In order to make this town as vital and pleaant as possible for the inhabitants, we undertook many differrent strategies.

In the central area, where the Tama stream flows, the stream was made as a symbol. On the southern edge of the gallery square water spews from a fountain in the pond, which flows underground for a time, then reemerges as a waterfall. It washes under a bridge and through rocks, then on through a small chasm, and finally again underground. It ultimately rises again, like a whale's spout, to end in the shopping mall.

But before we arrived at the above story, we had countless meetings with the planners, advertising agency, construction company, and various kinds of monument designers. The result was the establishment of a sequence flow and accompanying elements, their incorporation with the stream and pavement, rocks and greenery, and finally a sense of spatial completion.

At each point a monument was placed, one which lent identity to that particular space, while at the same time standing with the other elements as a coordinated, vital expression of the total design.

But the exhibition of elements if more than just a sequence of water, pavement, verdure, rocks, monument, bridge, etc. Rather it is an expression of the four seasons, in the greenery, and of the identities of different places, and finally as the theme of Park City. We believe that the unity of water and greenery, of space and human life, has been exemplified here in a single, total, integrated expression.

(Mikio Nakajima, Tooru Miyakoda)

5.札幌美術の森　21世紀への贈物,風雪と芸術

札幌芸術の森は自然と人間のかかわりの中から特に芸術活動を抽出して，人間と自然の接点を探ろうとするものである。21世紀へ向けて人間と自然，都市と自然とのかかわりを探る，今世紀末からの贈物となるべく札幌芸術の森は発想される。

このコンセプトを実現するために，札幌芸術の森は芸術の活動を目的とする施設とともに広範な人間行為を許容する柔軟な場－自然を持ち，庭は自然の中に凝縮する仕掛けとなって芸術が醸成される環境を創り出す。地域の文化から映し出された芸術活動の場は，現代人が希求する生活の規範を体験する場であり新たな創造への触発の場となって，独自の文化・芸術活動を生み出す輪廻と全地域的な波及効果を持つものとなる。こうした意味で札幌芸術の森の基盤は自然を凝縮した庭である。

都市化の時代に遠ざかった自然が再び豊かに人間の存在の場を作り，この中で営まれる様々な活動の風景が芸術活動にふさわしい環境を醸成する。季節の折々に自然と人間のかかわりを再認識する活動様式としてのイベントも開催され芸術活動はさらに活性化されていく。作庭はこのようなことがらを念頭に置きながら進められた。

北海道の自然は厳しい。工期2ケ年の月日はあっという間に過ぎた。時には台風の雨が来た。積雪のため工事を断念しなければならない事態も生じた。部分的には拙速のきらいのある部分も感じられるがオープン1年を経て，40万人を超える来訪者があったことは関係者一同，驚きであった。ランドスケープを創造する立場にあるわれわれ設計者の喜びであるとともに，この難儀な工事を施工するに当たって

惜しみ無い努力を傾注されたクライアントの「21世紀へ贈物を」の熱望がその輝かしい入場者数を象徴しているものと受け止めている。もちろん，施工を担当し黙々と働いて下さった関係者ご一同の並々ならぬご尽力があったことを忘れてはならない。紙上を借り厚くお礼申し上げたい。

札幌芸術の森は21世紀へ向けて第2，3期の整備が始められようとしている。反省，おしかり，思いがけないアクシデント，諸々の情念をエネルギーにして再び作庭ができればこれに勝る喜びはない。

21世紀に生きる人たちは，この芸術の森をどのように受け取ってくださるだろうか。それを楽しみにすべての人たちといっしょになって「札幌の庭」と取り組みたい。

(板谷邦夫)

a. 札幌芸術の森
b. 北海道札幌市
c. 札幌市
d. 渡辺亜紀夫
e. 板谷邦夫，大塚英典
f. 大富工業㈱，北土建設㈱，丸彦渡辺建設㈱，地崎工業㈱，岩田建設㈱
g. 提供:札幌市
j. 北海道開発コンサルタント㈱

a. LANDSCAPE OF SAPPORO ART PARK
b. Sapporo-shi, Hokkaido
c. Sapporo City
d. Akio Watanabe
e. Kunio Itaya, Eisuke Ohtsuka
f. OHTOMI KOGYO Co., Ltd., HOKUDO KENSETSU Co., Ltd., Maruhiko Watanabe Co., Ltd., CHIZAKI KOGYO Co., Ltd., Iwata Kensetsu Co., Ltd.
g. Sapporo City
j. HOKKAIDO ENGINEERING CONSULTANTS Co., Ltd.

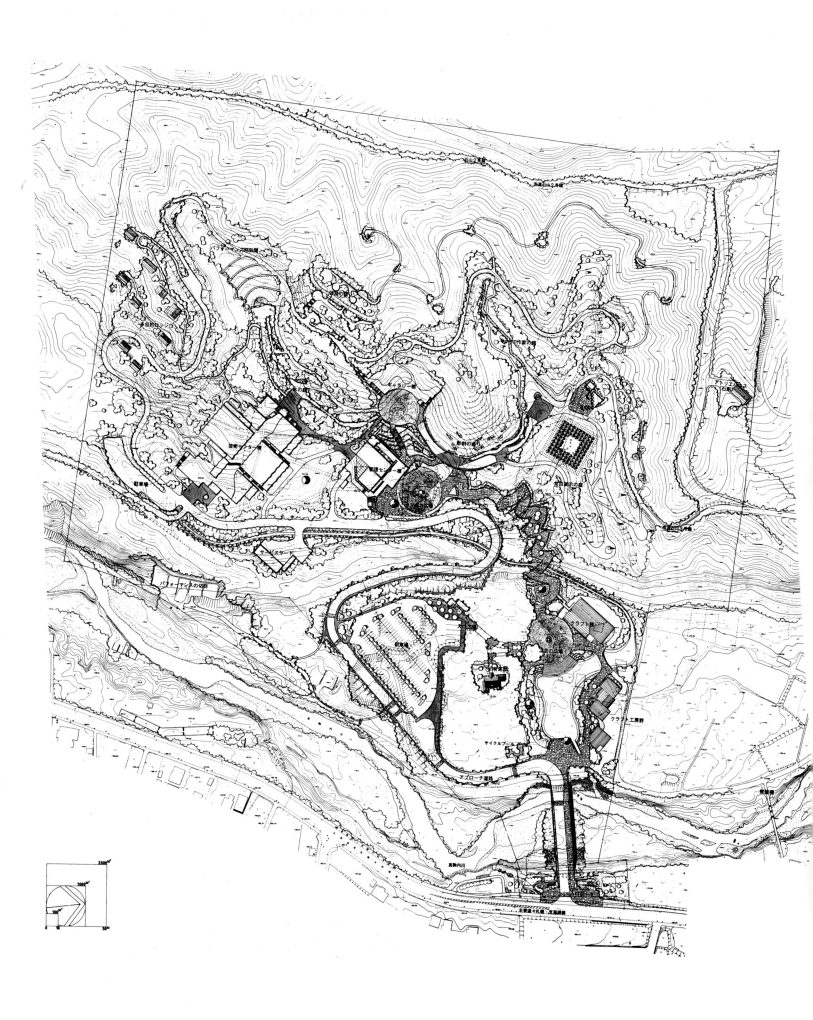

h. 工芸の広場から約20メートル昇る急斜面はつづら
　折の階段で結ぶ。樹木は全部残された。

h. The square is linked by a twenty meter, cypress
　covered stairway to the slope above.

f. 丸彦渡辺建設㈱
h. 工芸の広場は水面まで階段護岸によって広げられ
　る。水面左側は施工直後の石羽口護岸。
i. 石羽口護岸（ゴロ太石）／階段護岸（有明産硬石
　割石）

f. MARUHIKO WATANABE Co., Ltd.
h. The arts and crafts square reaches by steps to the
　bank of the water. To the left and just behind is the
　shore protection of riverstone and tuff.
i. Shore protection of Riverstone and turf, Ariake
　stone.

f. 丸彦渡辺建設㈱
h. 調整池を利用した水面に浮かぶマルタパンの作品。
　後方は工芸本館（左）と陶芸，ガラス工房。
i. 石造橋（有明産硬石）

f. Maruhiko Watanabe Co., Ltd.
h. The work of Marta Pan floats on the surface of this
　reservoir. The Central Hall is on the left, with
　ceramic and glass factory.

f. 丸彦渡辺建設㈱
h. 旧農家跡につくられた工芸の広場は屋敷林を利用
　し，緑濃い風景を構成した。
i. 床（隣接の採石場の骨材を用いた擬石平板）手す
　り（同じ割石による方形貼）

f. MARUHIKO WATANABE Co., Ltd.
h. The arts and craft center established on these
　ruins retained the woods of the old residence for
　riching greenery.
i. Floor and railings of pressed stone

37

f. 北土建設㈱
h. 芸術の森入り口橋梁。高欄は河岸に見える札幌軟石露頭をモチーフにした。正面は伊藤隆道氏の作品
i. 高欄（アルミ鋳物）／護岸（壮瞥産中硬石）／橋梁植栽（エリカ）

f. HOKUDO KENSETSU Co., Ltd.
h. Sapporo Art Park entrance. The high columns represent Sapporo's corp out stone, which can be seen at the river. The frontpiece is the work by Takamichi Itoh.
i. Cast aluminium (columns), stone(dyke), Erika (bridge plants)

f. 地崎工業㈱
h. 野外美術館入り口を構成する石造アーチ階段。シンボル彫刻はライモ・ウトリアイネン氏の作品
i. 石造アーチ階段（有明作品硬石）／右は札幌軟石露頭を模したコンクリート擬石ブロック

f. CHIZAKI KOGYO Co., Ltd
h. The arch stairway at the entrance to the museum.
i. Ariake stone, outcrop of Sapporo welded tuff

f. 丸彦渡辺建設㈱
h. 賑わいの広場になる工芸の広場の風景。床と壁面は暖色を基調に統一された。
i. 床は1メートル〜30センチの十勝御影化粧骨材の擬石平板と小舗石による同心円貼）

f. MARUHIKO WATANABE Co., Ltd.
h. A view of the soon to be bustling arts and crafts square.The floor and walls are united in a single, warm color tone.
i. The floor is a smooth surface made of Tokatsu granite and gravel.

f. 地崎工業㈱
h. 野外美術館の植生は貧弱で樹木は極力保存され
た。中央は澄川喜一氏の作品。
i. 札幌硬石割石／擬石ブロック

f. CHIZAKI KOGYO Co., Ltd
h. The Sculpture Garden with careful preserved
trees. The sculpture is by Kiichi Sumikawa.

f. 岩田建設㈱
h. シンボル広場の舗装パターン。工芸の広場と異な
り、白御影骨材を用いた擬石平板、小舗石使用。
i. 後方は雨水排水路のための有明産硬石野面石を
用いた石積

f. IWATA KENSETSU Co., Ltd.
h. Pattern for a symbol square.
i. Rain-resistant Ariake stone, natural surface stone

f. 丸彦渡辺建設㈱
h. 工芸の広場は休日毎に発表者のステージになる。
屋敷林が緑陰を提供する。
i. 照明灯（道産集成材）／サイン（ステンレス）／札幌
軟石台座

f. MARUHIKO WATANABE Co., Ltd.
h. On holidays the square becomes a stage for
announcements.
i. Lightstand, stainless steel sign, Sapporo Nansekis-
tone.

h. 札幌芸術の森の水面はすべてが雨水排水路が必
要な水路である。このカスケードも排水路となる。
i. 有明産硬石，十勝御影ゴロ太石／擬石平板ブロッ
ク

h. All available surfaces are uses for drainage here.
Even the cascade serves this purpose.
i. Ariake stone, Tokatsu granite stone, artificial
stone block

h. 野外美術館の中にある池と休憩所。中央の彫刻は佐藤忠良氏の作品「女・夏」。
i. 護岸（有明産中硬石）／護床（壮瞥産中硬石）／休憩所（化粧型枠コンクリート打放し

f. CHIZAKI KOGYO Co., Ltd.
h. The lake and rest place of The Sculpture Garden. The sculpture is Tyuryo Sato, "A Woman and Summer"

h. 沢沿いにわずかに残された貧弱な樹林も沢水、小径などによって変化に富む展示空間になる。

h. The plants along the marsh make for an ever-changing scene.

f. 地崎工業㈱
h. 野外美術館内の池周辺と丘。池の周辺には北海道ゆかりの彫刻家の作品が展示される。

f. CHIZAKI KOGYO Co., Ltd.
h. The sculpture works around the pond and hill include famous sculptor by connection with Hokkaido.

f. 地崎工業㈱
h. 野外美術館中央の広場。移動可能なベンチが設置されている。座る方向は規定しない。
i. 広場擬石平板舗装／ベンチ座板（ナラ材）／脚（札幌軟石）

f. CHIZAKI KOGYO Co., Ltd.
h. The central square of The Sculpture Garden, the furniture can be moved, so that benches can face in any direction.
i. Stone and nara wood (benches), artificial stone block pavement.

f. 岩田建設㈱
h. 野外美術館。地形はアレンジュレーションをつけ変化に富んだ自然な造成をしている。
i. ケンタッキーブリュグラス芝／園路（微砂利防塵舗装）

f. IWATA KENSETSU Co., Ltd.
h. The arrangement of The Sculpture Garden, reflects a richness and alterability.
i. Kentucky bluegrass turf, pavement preventing from dust

h. グループQの作品は野面石とトドマツを用いて丘陵地形につくられた。手前は柳原義達氏の作品。

h. The work of Artist Group Q is comprised of pine and stone, creating for of a hillock. In the forefront is Yoshitatsu Yanagihara work.

f. 地崎工業㈱
h. 作品の展示場所の地形は，作家との協議を重ね決定された。中央の彫刻は土谷武氏の作品。

f. CHIZAKI KOGYO Co., Ltd.
h. The artists have created works which conform to the natural surroundings. The center sculpture is by Takeshi Tsuchitani work.

f. 地崎工業㈱
h. 野外美術館。砂沢ビッキ氏作品の展示される丘の上から通りと広場を俯瞰する。
i. 広場(擬石平板舗装)／園路微砂利防塵舗装，ダスト舗装

f. CHIZAKI KOGYO Co., Ltd.
h. This sculpture by Bikky Sunazawa commands a view of the museum square and road from a top of the hill.
i. Artificial stone block pavement, pavement preventing from dust

Sapporo Forest of the Arts

A gift to the 21st century

The Sapporo Forest of the Arts seeks to take man's relation to nature and, particularly in the area of art, use it as a starting point for deepening man's involvement with nature. This is to be a gift of improvement in the relation between man and nature, and city and nature, to the twenty-first century.

In order to achieve this, Sapporo Forest of the Arts is a flexible facility which encourages the arts and a wide variety of human activity, a nature garden setting which allows for the artistic fermentation called creativity to take place. It is a facility which takes the flavor of regional culture and moves it into a place of artistic work, a kind of place which offers the living environment modern man is demanding. Here the sources of new creativity can be found for free, independent culture ; and this creative environment is now making itself felt, through its creative work, in regions far and wide.

The foundation of Sapporo Forest of the Arts is the garden, which is a condensed model of nature. The natural setting, which was forgotten during the urbanization age, has now returned to offer richness to human existence, and bring about in its multiplicity of activities a place where creativity can be nurtured. With the changing of the seasons and human development, the relation between nature and man is reaffirmed, and reflected in various artistic events which develop these changes.

The garden was initiated with this mind. Hokkaido's nature is severe, and the work of two years passed in the wink of an eye. Typhoon rains hit the project, and drifted snow forced work stoppage on occasion. In spite of feeling barely ready, the first year saw the coming of forty thousand visitors. Virtually everyone associated with the project was surprised.

As the facility moves into the twenty-first century, work is beginning on the second and third stages. In retrospect, there seems to be no way of improving on the start we have made.

(Kunio Itaya)

6.しながわ区民公園 臨海地区の活性化は世界の課題

古くから，品川区の工業地帯を結ぶ大動脈として機能してきた勝島運河は，近年の陸運の発達に伴い運河機能の重要性が低下し，さらに汚泥の堆積により船舶の航行にも支障をきたす事態があらわれ，その本来の機能がほとんど失われてしまった。

しながわ区民公園は新たな時代に対応し，これを再び区民の生活に結びついた都市生活機能に転換すべく，勝島運河を埋め立て造成し公園化したものである。

一般的にいって，船―水路が交通の手段であった時代には，海と陸をつなぐ結節点であった港湾施設は，鉄道や自動車が交通の手段となるや都市の中心は，水辺から離れ陸へ上がり，港湾及びその周辺は荒廃の一途をたどる結果となった。

こうした事態は日本だけでなく，世界の各地で問題になっており，臨海地区の再開発への関心が世界的な規模で高まっている。これらのプロジェクトに共通しているのは，荒廃化した港湾地区を再び〈人間〉を主役とした都市に再開発しようとしていることであり，情報化社会の主役となる産業，レクリエーション，住居機能を中心とした都市機能の複合化を図り，港湾地域に新たな魅力と活力を与えようとしている点である。

品川区では，区の重点施策の一つとして，昭和52年より5ケ年計画で，勝島運河の埋立事業を実施し，埋め立て完了に伴い57年より区民憲章制定記念公園として，しながわ区民公園を5ケ年で整備し，62年4月に完成した。

美しい水辺の再生

品川区では，古くから海とのかかわりが非常に密接な地域であり，独特な都市を形成した歴史を持っている。品川のこの地域特性が公園の性格づけに反映されることにより，必然的に公園は個性的なものとなろう。

従来の公園は，ともすれば地域の特性を軽視し，画一的な内容となる傾向があった。

このような傾向を排除し，公園をより個性的で地域に根をおろしたものとするために，美しい水辺の再生を焦点として設計を展開したのである。

（平松清房）

a.しながわ区民公園
b.東京都品川区
c.品川区土木部公園緑地課
d.平松清房
e.平松清房，榊原八朗，亀貝紘一郎，広田健一，
　栗原国男，原貴仁，渡辺義則
f.清水建設，小田急電鉄，井上工業他
g.北原美子（北井スタジオ），あい造園設計事務所
J.あい造園設計事務所

a. SHINAGAWA WARD PARK
b. Shinagawa-ku, Tokyo
c. Landscaping Section, Shinagawa Ward
d. Kiyofusa Hiramatsu
e. Kiyofusa Hiramatsu, Hachiro Sakakibara, Kenichi
   Hirota, Kunio Kurihara, Takahito Hara, Yoshinori
   Watanabe
f. SHIMIZU CORPORATYION, Odakyudentetsu Co.,
   Ltd.
g. Yoshiko Kitahara (Kitai Studio), Ai Landscape
   Planning Co., Ltd.
j. Ai Landscape Planning Co., Ltd.

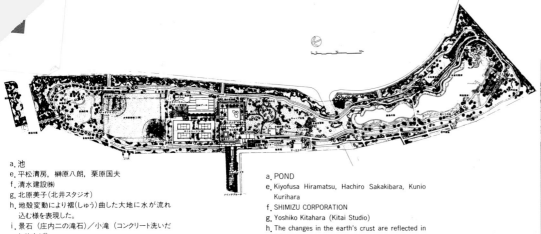

a. 池
e. 平松清房，榊原八朗，栗原国夫
f. 清水建設㈱
g. 北原美子（北井スタジオ）
h. 地殻変動により褶（しゅう）曲した大地に水が流れ込む様を表現した。
i. 景石（庄内二の滝石）／小滝（コンクリート洗いだし仕上げ）

a. POND
e. Kiyofusa Hiramatsu, Hachiro Sakakibara, Kunio Kurihara
f. SHIMIZU CORPORATION
g. Yoshiko Kitahara (Kitai Studio)
h. The changes in the earth's crust are reflected in this project.

a. 池
h. エコロジカルな水環境の創出を目指し，自然の海辺に近い構造とした。現在では多様な生物がこの池で生息している。
i. 池底（砂利敷き）

a. POND
e. Kiyofusa Hiramatsu, Hachiro Sakakibara, Kenichi Hirota, Kunio Kurihara
f. SHIMIZU CORPORATION
g. Yoshiko Kitahara (Kitai Studio)
h. This project reflects a concern for the ecological life of nearby seasides. Various lifeforms have taken hold here.
i. Sand, gravel

a. 池，モニュメント，洲浜
e. 平松清房，榊原八朗，広田健一，栗原国夫
f. 清水建設㈱
h. 眺めるだけの池でなく，人々が積極的に利用できるよう，洲浜と砂浜を大きく設けた。人も錨も景色の一部となる。
g. 北原美子（北井スタジオ）

a. POND, MONUMENT, SANDBANK
e. Kiyofusa Hiramatsu, Hachiro Sakakibara, Kenichi Hirota, Kunio Kurihara
f. SHIMIZU CORPORATION
g. Yoshiko Kitahara (Kitai Studio)
h. Not a pond merely to be looked at, this is something that people can participate in, and includes a beach and spit. People and anchors became parts of the scenry.

a. 流れ
e. 榊原八朗
f. ㈱小田急電鉄造園部
h. 岩盤の断層を激流が貫くさまを表現すべく，新たな石組みをこころみた。
i. 庄内二乃滝石

a. THE FLOW
e. Hachiro Sakakibara
f. Odakyudentetsu Co.,Ltd.
g. Yoshiko Kitahara (Kitai Studio), Ai Landscape Planning Co., Ltd., Kunio Kurihara
h. In this attempt to show the dramatic flow of rock a novel combination of stone was created.

a. 四阿
e. 榊原八朗
f. ㈱小田急電鉄造園部
g. 北原美子（北井スタジオ）
h. 親水性をより強調するために，四阿は池の中に設けた。
i. ヒノキ材

a. ARBOR
e. Hachiro Sakakibara
f. Odakyudentetsu Co., Ltd.
g. Yoshiko Kitahara (Kitai Studio)
h. To emphasize the affinity of water, this shelter was constructed over the water.

a. ディキャンプ場
e. 原貴仁
f. 井上工業㈱
g. 北原美子（北井スタジオ）
h. 都内の公園で焚火やバーベキューのできる数少ない場所。休日は家族づれで賑わう。

a. DAYCAMP
e. Takahito Hara
f. Inoue Kogyo Co., Ltd.
g. Yoshiko Kitahara (Kitai Studio)
h. One of the few places in the city where the family can go together and enjoy greenrey and a barbecue.

a. 忘れ物コーナー
e. 品川区公園緑地課
g. 北原美子（北井スタジオ）
h. 忘れ物コーナーは，あまり利用されないほうがよいのだが，連日大盛況。
i. スギ材／ビニールペイント塗り

a. A LOST AND FOUND
d. Kiyofusa Hiramatsu
e. Landscaping Section,Shinagawa Ward
g. Yoshiko Kitahara (Kitai Studio)
h. If possible it is better not to use the lost and found, but every day a great number of visitors gather here.
i. Japanese cedar

a. 石積み
e. 広田健一
f. 井上工業㈱
g. 北原美子（北井スタジオ）
h. 石積みは、城石垣をモチーフとした。
i. 白御影石／グラニットタイル

a. THE ROCK WALL
e. Kenichi Hirota
g. Yoshiko Kitahara (Kitai Studio)
h. This idea for this comes from castle construction
i. White granite and tile

a. 橋の親柱
e. 志津雅美
f. 志津雅美
g. 北原美子（北井スタジオ）
h. 百合鴎橋の親柱は江戸の心象風景を今に語り継ぐキーストーンである。
i. 庄内二乃滝石（本磨き）

a. CENTRAL BUTTRESS OF THE BRIDGE
e. Masami Sizu
g. Yoshiko Kitahara (Kitai Studio)
h. The Yurikamome Bridge central buttress is a reminder of the sprit and age of the Edo period.
i. Polished Stone

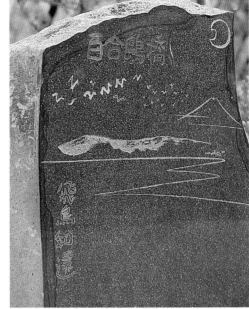

a. ロープ柵
e. 渡辺義則
f. 井上工業㈱
g. 北原美子（北井スタジオ）
h. この柵が朽ち果てる頃には植栽が柵の代わりを果たす。
i. スギ丸太／マニラロープ

a. ROPE PALISADE
e. Yoshinori Watanabe
f. Inoue Kogyo Co., Ltd.
g. Yoshiko Kitahara (Kitai Studio)
h. When the weir begins to rot, plants take over the job of the fence.
i. Japanese cedar and Manila rope

a. パーゴラ
e. 亀貝紘一郎，原貴仁
f. 井上工業㈱
g. 北原美子（北井スタジオ）
h. 噴水広場のフレームを形成するパーゴラ。春には〝藤の回廊〟となり人々の目を楽しませる。
i. コルテン鋼

a. A PERGOLA
e. Koichiro Kamegai, Takahito Hara
f. Inoue Kogyo Co., Ltd.
g. Yoshiko Kitahara (Kitai Studio)
h. This pergola is in the shape of the square. In spring it is covered with wisteria growth, a pleasing sight to the people.
i. Colton steel

a. 遊具
e. 平松清房，渡辺義則
f. 井上工業㈱
g. 北原美子（北井スタジオ）
h. 登る，飛ぶ，滑るなどの多様な活動が展開するよう木製遊具で構成したプレイグラウンドの遊具を設けた。

a. PLAYING OBJECT
e. Kiyofusa Hiramatsu, Yoshinori Watanabe
f. Inoue Kogyo Co., Ltd.
g. Yoshiko Kitahara (Kitai Studio)
h. A wooden playground built for climbing and jumping.

a. 水飲み
e. 栗原国夫
g. 北原美子（北井スタジオ）
h. 三つの石を組み合わせた水飲み。石の磨き面に周囲の景色が映し出される。
i. 黒御影石（本磨き）

a. DRINKING FOUNTAIN
e. Kunio Kurihara
g. Yoshiko Kitahara (Kitai Studio)
h. This fountain was created from three rocks. The polished surfaces reflect light from the surroundings.
i. Black granite.

a. 車止
e. 平松清房、渡辺義則
g. 北原美子（北井スタジオ）
h. 機能優先の車止めからの脱却を試みた。手型や顔
　などが彫刻されている。
i. 木曽石

a. WHELL BLOCK
e. Kiyofusa Hiramatsu, Yoshinori Watanabe
g. Yoshiko Kitahara (Kitai Studio)
h. An effort was made to create an excellent block.
　This one has the shape of a hand and face carved
　into it.
i. Flintstone.

a. 灰皿
e. 栗原国夫
h. 周辺環境との調和を考え、木製、スチール製、陶
　器の3タイプを場所により使いわけた。
i. ヒノキ材（オイルステイン）

a. ASHTRAY
e. Kiyofusa Hiramatsu, Kunio Kurihara
g. Yoshiko Kitahara (Kitai Studio)
h. The surroundings were considered in this design,
　which used wood, steel, and porcelain.
i. Oilstained cypress.

a. サイン
d. 平松清房
e. 品川区公園課
g. 北原美子（北井スタジオ）
h. サインデザインは、素朴で親しみのもてるものを目指
　し、デザインも"気を抜いた"ものとした。

a. SIGN
d. Kiyofusa Hiramatsu
e. Landscaping Section, Shinagawa Ward
g. Yoshiko Kitahara (Kitai Studio)
h. In this sign design, the appeal of the material was
　emphasized and the design kept unobtrusive.

Shinagawa Ward Park

Toward a new coastal community

From long ago the Katsushima Canal functioned as a major-artery of transport in the Shinagawa area. But with the advent of overland transport operation, the canal filled with silt and was hardly used for transport anymore. It no longer fulfilled its original function.

Now the Katsushima Canal has been filled in and renovated to become the Shinagawa Ward Park. Once again the water-way has been related to the lives of the people of Shinagawa.

The age of the canal and water transport came to an end with the coming of roads and rails, and the harbour saw the center of the city moving farther inland. The land along the port fell into disuse.

This phenomenon is taking place all over the world, and efforts to redevelop coast and port areas are widespread. With the industrialization and information-orientation of modern cities, these areas are now being regarded anew for their combined industrial, recreation and living potentials. With such wide appeal, planning of these areas is being undertaken

with considerable energy and foresight.

In Shinagawa ward a development effort of particular interest has been the filling and construction of the Katsushima Canal Park. Begun in 1982, the Shinagawa Ward Park was finally completed in April of 1987.

Beautiful water environs

From long ago Shinagawa ward has shared a special rela-tionship with the sea, and a unique historical development around it. Shinagawa has made efforts to make this park reflect the character of the region in the most natural way possible.

In the past there has been a tendency to make parks that were completely unconnected with the surrounding environ-ment. Henceforth there will be a new tendency to develop these projects in accordance with the special character of their locations, to use the 'roots' of a place to preserve beauty and original ambience.

(Kiyofusa Hiramatsu)

7.諏訪湖畔公園　人・自然・文化ここに出会う

諏訪湖畔公園は諏訪湖の湖畔を幅15メートルから50メートル、延長600メートルにわたって整備し、昭和61年「時の記念日」である6月10日にオープンした。

時計メーカー、セイコーエプソン社はその前身であった諏訪精工舎の創立から数えて創立満25周年を記念し公園を整備、これを諏訪市に寄付したのである。

クライアントは、公園整備を企業の単なる記念事業の一つに終わらせることなく、美しい湖をもう一度見つめ直し、湖を中心とする諏訪地域全体の将来を考えるきっかけにしていきたいと願っていた。

その基本的な企業の姿勢をデザインのベースとして諏訪地域の「人と自然」「人と文化」「人と人」が出会う、のびのびとした空間を創造することを目指した。このコンセプトに従って諏訪湖の大自然をバ

ックとした空間を人工的に作り過ぎないよう心がけ、季節や時の過ぎ行く中で多様に変化する自然と風景が織りなすドラマの推移をイメージし具体的な環境デザインとエレメントで展開してみた。

立地が河川地域であることによるもろもろの規制や制約、苛酷な自然条件の2点は大きな問題であった。規制問題は関係各位の有形無形のご尽力によって解決され、最終的な形にまとめあげることができた。今もなお深く感謝している。

しかし、諏訪湖の自然は厳しい。寒暖の差も激しい。冬季、湖上を吹き抜けてくる寒風は肌を刺し、工事の進捗や植栽にも重大な影響を与えずにはおかなかった。また、軟弱な地盤であるためその対策として基礎工事には十分留意したのであるが、現在もなお若干の地盤沈下が見られる。

完成後、この公園は若い人たちで埋まった。「諏訪

にはこんなにたくさんの若者がいたのか」、それが地元の多くの人たちの素朴な驚きであった。

「人と人との出会いの場」として公園を整備すれば人々が湖に出てきてくれるに違いない。設計者の確信はものの見事に的中したのである。

この計画と前後して湖岸にサイクリングロード、ポケットパークの計画が立案され、市民の間からも湖畔を自主的に有効利用しようとする積極的な提案も出されるなど、地域を活性化するインパクトとして大きな役割を果たしている。

公園を訪れる人たちの年齢はさまざまである。すべての人にとってこの公園が「出会いの広場」として、あるいは「人生の長い時を心に刻みこんでいく場」として愛され親しまれていくことを切に願ってやまない。

（戸田芳樹）

a. 諏訪湖畔公園
b. 長野県諏訪市
c. セイコー・エプソン㈱
d. 黒川紀章、北村文雄、亀山章
e. 小口基実、島川清史、伊藤直博、㈱戸田芳樹＋風景計画、地福由紀、奈木政幸、戸田芳樹、小峰貴芳
f. 竹中・清水共同企業体
g. 伊藤直博
j. ㈱戸田芳樹＋風景計画

a. SUWA LAKESIDE PARK
b. Suwa-shi, Nagano
c. Seiko Epson Co., Ltd.
d. Kisho Kurokawa, Fumio Kitamura, Akira Kameyama
e. Motomi Oguchi, Kiyosi Shimakawa, Naohiro Ito, Toda Yoshiki & Fukei Keikaku Associates, Yuki Jlfuku, Masayuki Nagi, Yoshiki Toda, Takayoshi Komine
f. Takenaka, SHIMIZU, J. V.
j. Toda Yoshiki & Fukei Keikaku

a. モニュメント

e. モニュメント造形・戸田芳樹

h. 中央にそびえる高さ12メートルのステンレスのモニュメントは、7年に一度行われる諏訪人社の奇祭「御柱」のイメージを時間の輪廻として現代風に解釈してデザインした。2本の柱のスリットに落日の風景を写しだし、永遠の時の流れに対する祈りと畏敬を封じこめた。
足元を諏訪湖の全体図で形どり、その中心にモニュメントを置き、そのまわりに十二支をデザインして時間の流れを表現した。

a. MONUMENT

h. The twelve meter stainless steel tower which rises in the center is a modern design realization of transmigration for the 'Pole' festival, which occurs in the Suwa Shrine every seven years. Two poles, reflecting the scenery of the setting sun, stand as a prayer to the eternal flow of time.
At the base is a model of the region, with the poles rising from the center and twelve arms radiating out, representing the flow of time. Design by Yoshiki Toda.

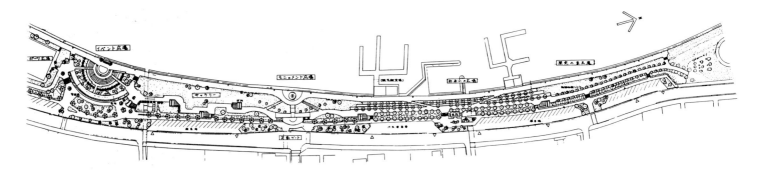

a. イベント広場

h. この広場は湖にある初島を軸線上に配置し、二重のステージを設けた。湖側は木製のデッキを湖上に突き出し、展望デッキを兼ねている。

a. EVENT SQUARE

h. This square stands in a direct line to a nearby island, and contains two stages. The lakeside stage is built of wood and extends out over the water, doubling as an observation deck.

a. 四阿

h. 公園に隣接している片倉館は千人風呂で有名である。ここのファサードをモチーフとしてデザインした。5ケ所に分かれている四阿はそれぞれ色彩を変え、変化を持たせた。

a. THE ARBORS

h. Next to the Park is the Katakura inn, famous for its large bath. The arbors were designed with facade as a motif. They are located in five places, where they imparted their own particular color and variety to the settings.

a. 歴史の並木道
e. 鍛鉄造形・小峰貴芳
h. 諏訪地域の自然，歴史などを鍛鉄造形で表現した。クライアントであるセイコーエプソン社にちなんだアナログ型の時計は「時計のふるさと諏訪」をイメージして制作されている。

a HISTORY'S ROW OF TREES
h. Metal workings which represents the Suwa region's history and nature, these were designed for Seiko-Epson along the lines of the analog clock. It appropriately represents 'Suwa, town of time-pieces'. Design by Takayoshi Komine.

Suwa Lakeside Park

A meeting place for people, nature, and culture

Suwa Lakeside Park occupies a width fifteen to fifty meters along the lakeside, and extends for some six hundred meters. It was constructed in 1986 and opened on 'Time Day', the tenth of June, 1986.

Seiko-Epson Co., Ltd., originally Suwa Seikosha, counted a full twenty-five years since its establishment, and made the park a contribution to Suwa city on this occasion.

The client wanted this park to be more than just a simple memorial construction project. It was hoped that through it the beauty of the lake would be better appreciated, and that the park, as a center of the region, would be reviewed in future years.

Against this basic corporate backdrop a design base was realized which created a space in the Suwa region where many more meetings of 'man and nature,' 'man and cultrure,' and 'man and man' could take place. In accord with this concept the natural setting was used as a backdrop, and artificial construction was not overdone. The natural changes of season and nature were emphasized through environmental design which was carefully woven in, bringing out the drama of the setting.

An industrial location by a river means severe environmental restrictions of two kinds. These problems were ironed out with the help of various officials, and we owe them great thanks.

But Suwako-lake is a harsh environment, with extreme ranges in temperature. The winter winds blowing off the lake cut to the bone, and progress in planting trees was made with difficulty. The soill around the lake is soft, and considerable care was taken here, as well. A slight amount of sinking in the area has nonetheless occured.

After completion the park was buried in young people. There were exclamations from all around——no one had known there were so many youths in Suwa. As meeting place of people the park was a beautiful success. The planner's idea was right on the mark.

Plans for a cycling road to go along with the pocket park have been put forth, and members of the community are proposing ways of utilizing the lake more actively. The park is bringing about far greater activity in the region.

People of all ages are visiting the park, and we sincerely hope that everyone is overjoyed with it as a meeting place, a place where 'long lifes come into touch with the spirit.

(Yoshiki Toda)

8.大井ふ頭お台場海浜公園　ヘドロの東京湾に甦った自然の渚

　公園の名称となった「お台場」は江戸末期，開港を迫る黒船の出現にあわてた徳川幕府が東京湾内に設けた6基の砲台のうちの一つであり，それを象徴的に取り入れたことから名付けられたものである。

　この地は，国内や海外の各地から運ばれてきた木材の貯木場であり，久しく使用が中止されていた。自然を回復させその保全とレクリエーションの場として「生きた波打際」を蘇らせる，これが設計の最大のテーマであった。

　大都会の周辺に緑豊かな自然を取り戻すことの難しさはことさら語るまでもない。海浜の自然環境を蘇生するには，眼で見える可視的範囲にとどまらず，不可視の部分である水面下や土壌をいかに活性させるかが重大な課題であった。

　潮の干満によって生じる干潟はイソシギやチドリなどの餌場となり，潮だまりには取り残された魚やカニなどが観察できるよう，生物環境を豊かにする工夫が凝らされている。このため莫大な予算をヘドロや沈んだ木材の除去および安山岩などによる磯浜の構築に投入し，海底の自然生態系が文字通り自然に定着していくよう設計されている。

　現在見られるこの景観は自然に残されていたのではなく自然生態系の科学的な調査研究に基づく設計によってすべてを造成した「人工の渚」である。その甲斐あって干潟には設計どおりゴカイが生息し，潮だまりには小魚が泳いでいる。

　こうした努力の結果，イソシギ，アジサシ，ユリカモメなどの水辺を彩る野鳥の群れが飛び交い，餌をついばむ光景が観察されその数がしだいに増えつつある。

　海浜植物の植栽も同様である。東京港に生育している海浜植物の分布状況の基礎的データからその土壌条件までを徹底的に調査し設計に当たった。

　ハマヒルガオやコウボウムギなどは港内から移植し，ツルナ，ハマエンドウ，ギョウギシバは種子蒔き，イソギク，ハマニンニク，ハマゴウ，キリンソウ，オニヤブマオ，ハマギク，ハマカンゾウ，ワダンなどは鉢仕立てて植栽した。その植栽ゾーニングとしてシャリンバイ，トベラ，ハマヒサカキなどの低木の他，ツワブキ，ハマギク，ワダンなどの岩場や崖に生育する植物とハマヒルガオ，ハマナス，スイセン，コウボウムギなど磯や砂浜に生育する植物を使い分け岩場と砂浜が一体化する景観を演出した。

　東京湾の自然は埋立などによって減少の一途をたどっているが，植物園以外でこれだけの量と種類の海浜植物を用いた例がなく，珍しい存在になっている。

　公園の全体構成は，海浜保全水域ゾーン，レクリエーション水域ゾーン，海上バス運航ゾーン，広場・緑地・散策ルートゾーンなどに分かれている。

　都心から近いこともあって，潮干狩り，磯遊び，ウインドサーフィンなどのレクリエーションが盛んに行われており，公園建設の狙いであった「東京湾に自然の渚を……」の目的は達成されたようである。

　この事例が，今後の埋立地や海浜公園の建設のあり方についていささかの参考になれば幸いである。

(堀越千里，杉田　章)

a. 大井ふ頭お台場海浜公園
b. 東京都港区
c. 東京都港湾局海上公園課
d. 小林治人
e. 小林治人，堀越千里，宮崎保郎，渋谷卓夫，杉田章
f. 五洋建設㈱
g. 堀越千里，杉田章，ミッキー・中島
j. 東京ランドスケープ研究所

a. OHI PIER CENTRAL SEASIDE PARK
b. Minato-ku,Tokyo
c. Seaside Park Department, Port and Harbor Bureau, Tokyo Metropolitan Government.
d. Haruto Kobayashi
e. Chisato Horikoshi, Yasuro Miyazaki, Takuo Shibuya, Akira Sugita
g. Chisato Horikoshi, Akira Sugita, Mikky, Nakajima
j. Tokyo Landscape Research & Development.

a. 総合案内板
d. 小林治人
e. 堀越千里
g. 堀越千里，ミッキー・中島
h. 屋根を杉皮葺とし，和風仕立てとした。
i. 杉材／銅板

a. COMPREHENSIVE GUIDEPOST
e. Chisato Horikoshi
g. Chisato Horikoshi Mikky. Nakajima
h. Cedar bark, in the Japanese style.

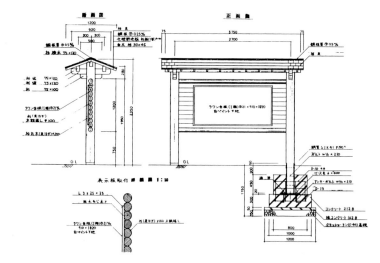

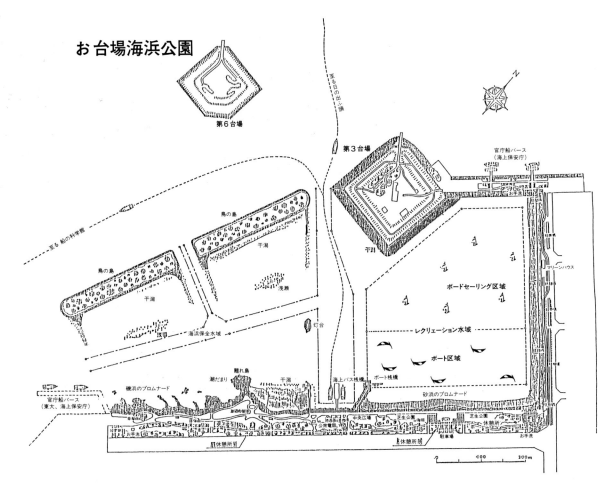

お台場海浜公園

a. 磯浜
e. 宮崎保郎
g. 杉田章, ミッキー・中島
h. 真壁の護岸を人間や生物にとって親しめる護岸に
　整備した。
i. 安山岩／硬質砂岩

a. A PEBBLESTONE BEACH
e. Yasuro Miyazaki
g. Akira Sugita Mikky Nakajima
h. A waterbreak that man and animal can find attrac-
　tive.
i. Stone

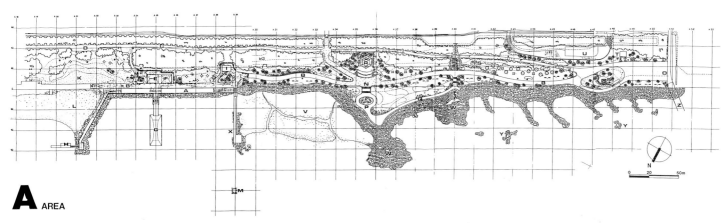

A AREA

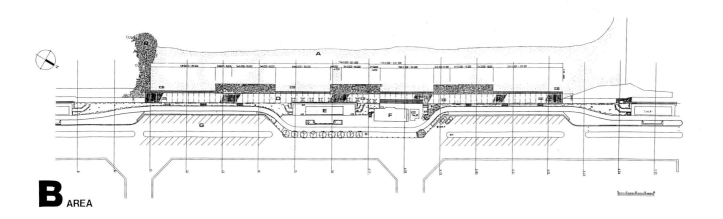

B AREA

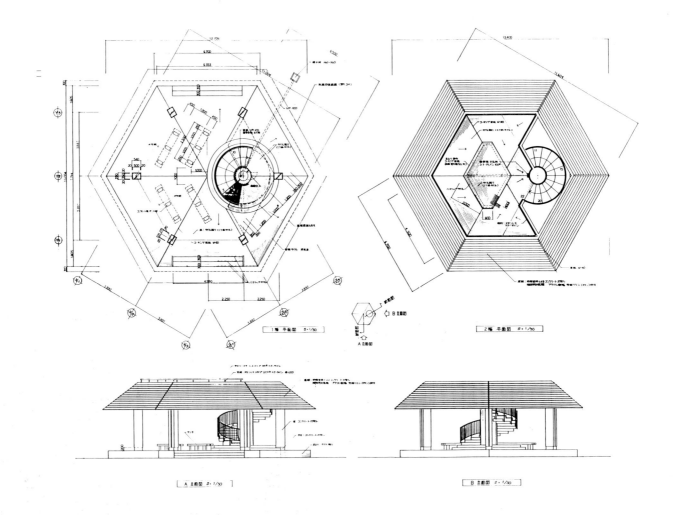

1階 平面図 ﾇ・1/30

2階 平面図 ﾇ・1/30

A 立面図 ﾇ・1/30

B 立面図 ﾇ・1/30

a. 展望台と休憩所
e. 渋谷卓夫
g. 杉田章
h. 螺旋階段を登る屋上が展望台で一階は休憩所。
i. 鉄筋コンクリート

a. OBSERVATION DECK AND RESTING PLACE.
e. Takuo Shibuya
g. Akira Sugita
h. The spiral stairway leads up from the restplace to
   the rooftop observation deck.
i. Reinforced concrete

a. 乱杭
e. 宮崎保郎
f. 五洋建設㈱
g. 杉田章
h. 材木を連結する杭を野鳥たちが安全に休息できる
　場として再びランダムに打ち直した。

a. PALISADE
e. Yasuro Miyazaki
f. Goyo Kensetsu Co., Ltd.
g. Akira Sugita
h. This fence was built between posts in a way that
would attract birds.

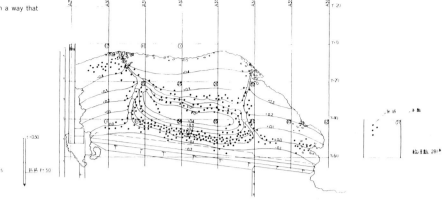

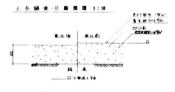

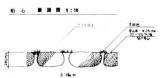

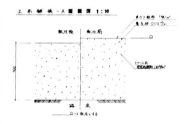

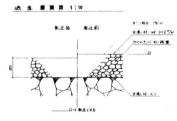

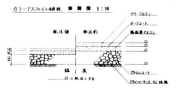

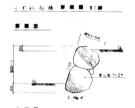

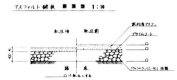

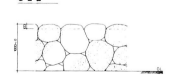

a. 土系舗装
e. 杉田章
g. 堀越千里
h. 不純物が混入されていない砂にセメント系安定剤
　を混入、表面に貝殻を散布、海浜の道を演出し
　た。

a. SOIL PAVEMENT
e. Akira Sugita
g. Chisato Horikoshi
h. This walk was built using cement and clean sand,
and covreted with seashells to make an appropriate and longlasting surface.

a. 自然石階段
d. 小林治人
e. 杉田章
g. 杉田章
h. やがて繁茂する海浜植物を意識して，荒々しい階段とした。
i. 安山岩

a. NATURAL STONE STEPS
e. Akira Sugita
g. Akira Sugita
h. These steps are rugged and evocative of the plantlife which has taken hold and flourished.
i. Anzan stone

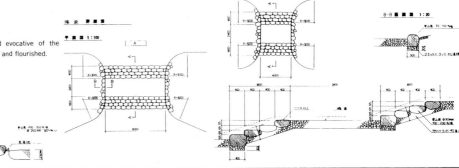

a. ボートデッキ
d. 小林治人
e. 宮崎保郎
g. 堀越千里
h. 東京湾内で初めてのボートデッキである。
i. アオモリヒバ材

a. BOAT DECK
e. Yasuro Miyazaki
g. Chisato Horikoshi
h. Tokyo bay's first boat deck.
i. Aomori Hiba wood

a. 野外卓　　　　　　a. OUTDOOR TABLE
e. 杉田章　　　　　　e. Akira Sugita
g. 堀越千里　　　　　f. Chisato Horikoshi
i. ヒノキ／スギ　　　i. Cypress and cedar

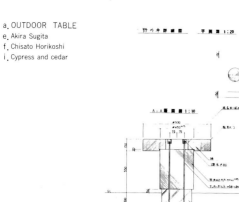

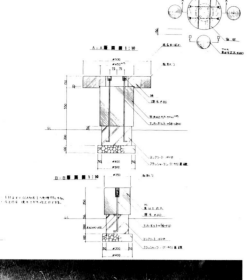

a. 丸太ベンチ　　　　a. LOG BENCH
d. 小林治人　　　　　e. Chisato Horikoshi
e. 堀越千里　　　　　g. Chisato Horikoshi
g. 堀越千里　　　　　i. Stripped cedar
i. 皮はぎ杉丸太

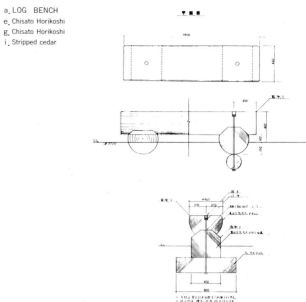

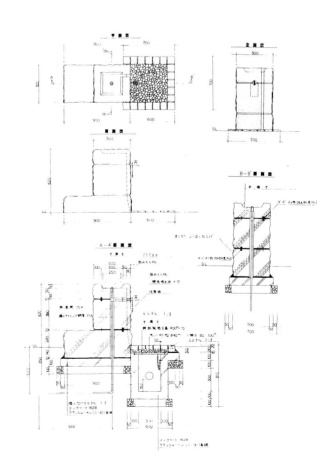

a. 足洗い場　　　　　　　　　　　a. FOOT WASHING BASIN
e. 堀越千里　　　　　　　　　　　e. Chisato Horikoshi
g. 堀越千里　　　　　　　　　　　g. Chisato Horikoshi
h. お台場の景観に調和するように自然石を用いた。　h. Made from natural stones, to fit the landoscape.
i. 本御影石（コブ出し仕上げ）　　i. Granite

Ohi Pier Central Seaside Park

A natural beach for Tokyo bay

The park name of 'O-Daiba' was taken for this area, where the black ships frist appeared. The Tokugawa goverment hurried to set up six gun implacements, one of which was here. The name 'O-Daiba' recalls this event.

This area was originally where lumber was brought from around the world and stored, but was long ago abandoned and left in ruins. The creation of a new shoreline with a protected natural environment has a major theme in planning.

Nothing needs to be explained concerning the difficulty of returning abundant greenery to the areas around major cities. Bringing the environs of the shore back to life involves more thought, than just that which can be seen. There is the world beneath the water which must also be reawakened.

Observation of the tidal regions, where plover and snipe feed on crabs and fish in the shallows, has been one area where efforts to enrich environment have been concentrated. The removal of sludge and the rebuilding of the coastline with andesite has been undertaken to ensure the sealife will thrive naturally.

What can now be seen here is not a natural, preserved coastline, but one which has been brought back to life completely through study, planning and reconstruction efforts. Now, as planned, lugworms live and small fish swim in these tidal flats. As a result of this seagulls, terns, and shrike are now seen flocking to the area and feeding in ever greater numbers.

The pattern has been the same with floral life. Studies have been made on the seashore plantlife, and date gathered on soil makeup and distribution, ending with planning based on thorough analysis.

Plants such as bindweed and wheatgrass were moved from the harbour, and spinach, pea, and *gyogi* grass was planted. Chrysanthemum, wild garlic, wild pepper, orange stonecrop, lilies and other flowers were planted in pots. Shrubs such as Eurya Japonica were used for ground cover, and silverleaf and chrysanthemums were placed in rocky areas. Bindweed and sweet briar and narcissus were planted to join together both rocky and sand environments in a single panorama.

Refilling Tokyo bay has led to great decreases the shoreline life, and outside other floral parks this natural coastline plantlife is impressive both in variety and volume. It is a very rare place indeed.

The park is structured to serve as a water zone, over-sea bus terminal, square, green area and strolling area.

As an area which is close to the city it serves as a recreation zone and tidal preservation environment, with playgrounds and windsurfing in abundance. The aim of creating "a natural beach for Tokyo" was achieved.

This project will hopefully serve as an example and reference for future lanfill development projects.

(Chisato Horikoshi, Akira Sugita)

9.ペリー公園・木製遊具

子供たちに贈るロマンへの船出

江戸時代の末期, 欧米列強諸国の日本開港論が高まる中で, 1853年7月8日和親開港を求めて投錨しペリー提督が上陸したのがペリー公園付近の久里浜海岸であった。

ペリー公園は, このペリー来航100周年を記念して, 横須賀市が昭和29年にモニュメント広場として整備したものであるが, 昭和60年に市制80周年記念事業として新たに改修整備がなされた。

本公園の面積は0.7haと記念公園としてはその規模は小さいものであるが,「ペリー上陸記念碑」を中心に, ペリー記念館, 遊具広場などがコンパクトにまとまったものになっている。

黒船をイメージした船形

この公園の動的な広場として, 木製遊具の遊び場がある。ここに黒船をイメージした船形の木製遊具と, 砂場を海に見立て, 近くに岬の灯台を表す砦を配置した。

これらの木製遊具は, 子供達が海原に船出する船乗りや, 灯台守になった気分で海にそのロマンを馳せ, 歴史を考え, 豊かな創造力が培われるように考えた。

また, この公園は海に隣接し常に潮風に当たるため, 鉄製を避け, サビの出ない, 手に温もりが感じられる木製遊具を選んだ。規模は小さくても夢は大きく膨らむ。

母親に連れられてきた内気な子供が, 怖ず怖ずと木製遊具の船に登る。周囲の子供達を気にとめながら, しかしやがてベンチに座っている母親に向かってそっと手を振る。

時間が去る。また子供が母親に向かって微笑みながら手を大きく振り, 今度は声をかける。潮風に向かって冒険心をそそるのだろうか……。あたかも船長になった気分で……。子供達からの爽やかなメッセージが伝わってくる。

(浅見信夫)

a. ペリー公園・船と灯台の遊具
b. 神奈川県横須賀市
c. 横須賀市
d. 森緑地設計事務所
e. 浅見信夫
f. 双葉造園土木㈱
g. 鹿子丈夫
i. 木材（特殊防腐処理したダグラスモミ）
j. ㈱創研

a. PERRY PARK PLAYGROUND, SHIP & LIGHT-HOUSE EQUIPMENT
b. Yokosuka-shi, Kanagawa
c. Yokosuka City
d. Mori Landscape Architects Inc.
e. Nobuo Asami
f. Futaba Zoen Co., Ltd.
g. Takeo Kanoko
i. Wood(wrather resistant Douglas Fir)
j. Souken Co., Ltd.

Perry Park Wooden Playground Square

A gift of sailing fantasies to the children

On July 8, 1853, even while the arguments to open Japan were increasing in America and Europe, Commodore Perry's ships dropped anchor and the commander came ashore on the Kurihama Coast, at a point nearby what is now Perry Park.

Perry Park was built to commemorate the one hundredth year anniversary of the first visit, when in 1954 the city of Yokosuka built a square and erected a monument. In 1985, the eightieth year of the city's municipality, rennovation of the memorial took place.

The area of the park is only 0.7 hectares, which is small for a park, but the monument to Perry's first footsteps in Japan, the museum, and the playground are neatly and compactly arranged in this area.

'Image of the Black Ships'

In this park is a dynamic playground with wooden rides, one of which is modeled on the 'Black Ship', another being a fort that resembles the lighthouse on the point nearby.

Playing on these creations by the water-sailing to sea on their ship, guarding the land from their lighthouse——children fantasize about the sea, relive history, and develop their imaginations.

In this location wood construction was preferred to metal, which would rust, and also does not have the warm, intimate feel. Although the scale of the project was small, our dreams were great.

Even shy children come with their mothers to this park and fearfully climb the wooden ship. They watch the other children for a time, then finally turn and wave to their mothers. After a time they turn again and wave broadly, this time smiling brightly, sensing perhaps the great adventure that lies ahead on the salty main. They have become captains and they are sending their last, energetic farewell.

(Nobuo Asami)

Elements & Total Concept of

URBAN LANDSCAPE DESIGN

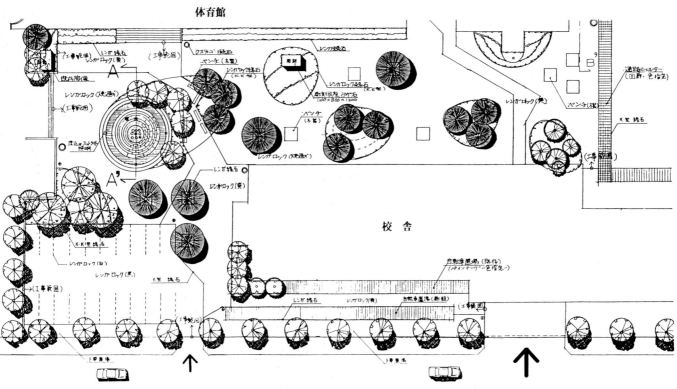

a. 沼津学園高校キャンパス・ペーブパターン
b. 静岡県沼津市
c. 沼津学園高等学校　是村恵三
d. 上法武文（鹿島建設・横浜支店）
e. 都田徹，横田博，鍛治貴夫，（景観設計研究所）
f. 鹿島建設，東建工業，アズミック，久保田鉄工
g. 廣田治雄，都田徹
h. 高校生活の思い出となるような暖かさ，明るさそして
　　外部空間での生活体験としてのペーブメントとした。
i. レンガブロック／ピンコロ／リョウワタイル
j. 景観設計研究所・都田 徹

a. NUMAZU GAKUEN HIGH SCHOOL CAMPASS
　　PAVEMENT PATTERN
b. Numazu-shi, Shizuoka
c. Keizo Koremura (Numazu Gakuen High school)
d. Takefumi Joho (KAJIMA Corporation Co., Ltd.,
　　Yokohama)
e. Tooru Miyakoda, Hiroshi Yokota, Takao Kaji,
　　(Total Environmental Design Office, Tokyo)
f. KAJIMA Corporation Co., Ltd., Token Kogyo,
　　Azumikku, KOTOBUKI Lt d.
g. Haruo Hirota, Tooru Miyakoda
h. Outside pavement design is meant to recall bright
　　and warm memorise of high school days
i. Block, pincoro, Ryouwa tile
j. Total Environmental Design Office, Tokyo, Tooru
　　Miyakoda

a. 沼津学園高校キャンパス・ペーブパターン
b. 静岡県沼津市
c. 沼津学園高等学校　是村恵三
d. 上法武文（鹿島建設・横浜支店）
e. 都田徹，横田博，鍛治貴夫，（景観設計研究所）
f. 鹿島建設，東建工業，アズミック，久保田鉄工
g. 廣田治雄，都田徹
h. 高校生活の思い出となるような暖かさ，明るさそして
　　外部空間での生活体験としてのペーブメントとした。
i. レンガブロック／ピンコロ／リョウワタイル
j. 景観設計研究所・都田 徹

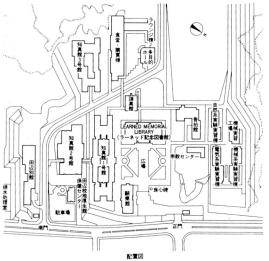

配置図

a. 同志社大学田辺キャンパスのペーブパターン
b. 京都市田辺町
c. 同志社大学
d. ㈱日建設計
f. 大林組・戸田建設・熊谷組・大成建設・フジタ工
　業共同企業体
i. INAX タイル
j. ㈱ＩＮＡＸ

a. DOSHISYA UNIVERSITY, TANABE CAMPUS
　PAVEMENT PATTERN
b. Tanabe-cho, Kyoto
d. NIKKEN SEKKEI Ltd.
f. Ohbayashi-Gumi, Ltd. Toda Construction Co., Ltd.
　Kumagai-Gumi, Co., Ltd., TAISEI Corporation,
　Fujita Kogyo Co., Ltd., J. V.
j. INAX Co., Ltd.

a. 秋田ターミナルビルのペーブパターン
b. 秋田県秋田市
c. JR 東日本
d. JR 東日本
e. 竹中工務店・熊谷組 J. V.
f. 岡元タイル
g. 佐藤勉
i. 磁器質無釉タイル
j. ダントー㈱

a. PAVEMENT, AKITA TERMINAL BUILDING
b. Akita-shi, Akita
c. East Japan Railway Company
d. East Japan Railway Company
f. Takenaka Koumuten Co., Ltd., Kumagai-Gumi Co.,
　Ltd., J. V., Okamoto Tile
g. Tsutomu Sato
i. Porcelain unglazed tile
j. Danto Co., Ltd.

a. 安佐北高校のペーブパターン
b. 広島市
c. 広島県
d. 都市建築研究所
f. 大成建設, 広島窯業
g. 旺映社
j. ダントー㈱

a. ASAKITA HIGH SCHOOL PAVEMENT PAT-
   TERN
b. Hiroshima-shi, Hiroshima
c. Hiroshima Pre.
d. Urbanicts Architects
f. TAISEI Corporation Hiroshima Yogyo Co., Ltd.
g. Ohei-sha
j. DANTO Co., Ltd.

a. 神戸 UCC 博物館のペーブメント
b. 兵庫県神戸市
c. U. C. C., Co., Ltd.
d. 竹中工務店
e. 黒瀬歩行
g. 仲佐写真事務所
h. 水を浸透するセラミックタイルを貼り地下水が確保
   できるようにした
i. ダイチブレースタイル
j. ㈱ダイチ

a. KOBE UCC MUSEUM
b. Kobe-shi, Hyogo
c. UCC Corporation
d. Takenaka Koumuten Co., Ltd.
e. Tadayuki Kurose
g. T. Nacàsa & Partners
h. Using a permeable tile making water seep down
   into the earth
j. DAICHI Co., Ltd.

a. アークヒルズ外溝
b. 東京都港区
c. 森ビル㈱
d. 入江・三宅設計事務所，環境設計研究室
e. リョーワ工業㈱
f. 鹿島道路・大成建設・清水建設・竹中工務店共
　　同企業体
g. 竹林龍三郎
i. 御影質磁器石材（人口御影石）／サンセラミカゲ
j. リョーワ工業㈱

a. ARK HILLS BUILDING PAVEMENT PATTERN
b. Minato-ku, Tokyo
c. MORI BUILDING Co., Ltd.
d. Irie Miyake Architects & Engineers, Environmental
　　Engineering Consultants Co., Ltd.
e. RYOWA INDUSTRY Co., Ltd.
f. KAJIMA ROAD Corporation, TAISEI Corporation,
　　SIMIZU CORPORATION, Takenaka Koumuten Co.,
　　Ltd., J. V.
g. Ryuzaburo Takebayashi
j. RYOWA INDUSTRY Co., Ltd.

a. 東芝ビルのペーブパターン
b. 東京都港区
c. 東芝㈱
d. 清水建設㈱
f. 清水建設・鹿島建設共同企業体, 不二窯業・丸西タイル・日本窯業
g. 千代田
i. せっ器質無釉タイル
j. ダントー㈱

a. TOSHIBA BUILDING PAVEMENT PATTERN
b. Minato-ku, Tokyo
c. Toshiba Corporation
d. SIMIZU CORPORATION
f. SIMIZU CORPORATION, KAJIMA Corporation, J. V., MARUNISHI Tile Co., Ltd., NIHON YOGYO Co., Ltd., FUJI YOGYO Co., Ltd.
g. Chiyoda
i. Stoneware unglazed tile
j. DANTO Co., Ltd.

a. 千葉ポートタワーのペーブパターン
b. 千葉県千葉市
c. 千葉県
d. ㈱日建設計
f. 竹中工務店
h. 黄色とブルーによって若さと未来へ向かって躍動する港湾施設機能の動的な空間を表現した。
j. ㈱INAX

a. CHIBA PORT TOWER PAVEMENT PATTERN
b. Chiba-shi, Chiba
c. Chiba Pre.
d. NIKKEN SEKKEI Ltd.
f. Takenaka Koumuten Co., Ltd.
h. A yellow and blue representation that recalls activity of the port and bay.
j. INAX Co., Ltd.

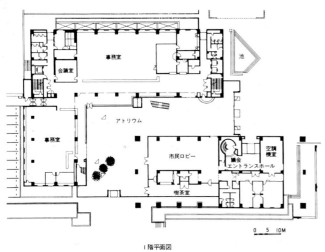

1階平面図

a. 南足柄市庁舎のペーブパタン
b. 神奈川県南足柄市
c. 南足柄市
d. 佐藤武夫設計事務所
f. 清水建設㈱
j. ㈱INAX

a. MINAMI ASHIGARA MUNICIPAL OFFICE
   PAVEMENT PATTERN
b. Minami-ashigara-shi, Kanagawa
c. Construction Department, Minami-ashigara City
d. Satow, Architects & Engineers
f. SHIMIZU CORPORATION
j. INAX Co., Ltd.

a. 愛媛県民文化会館のペーブパターン
b. 愛媛県松山市
c. 愛媛県
d. 丹下健三・都市建築設計研究所
f. 鹿島建設・西松建設・野間工務店共同企業体
h. 幾何学紋様のパターンを連続させ広がりを表現。一定の方向性を与えることによりさらに広がりを強調した。
j. ㈱INAX

a. EHIME KENMIN CULTURAL HALL PAVEMENT PATTERN
b. Matsuyama-shi, Ehime
c. Ehime Pre.
d. Kenzo Tange Associates Urbanicts Architects
f. KAJIMA Corporation, NISHIMATSU KENSETSU Co., Ltd., Noma-koumuten Co., Ltd. J. V.
h. Expressing an expanding geometric pattern rather than any set form
j. INAX Co., Ltd.

a. 松江総合文化センターのペーブパターン
b. 島根県松江市
c. 松江市
d. ㈱日建設計・建築技術センター共同企業体
f. 鹿島建設・松江土建共同企業体
j. ㈱INAX

a. MATSUE CITY CULTURAL CENTER PAVEMENT PATTERN
b. Matsue-shi, Shimane
c. Matsue City
d. NIKKEN SEKKEI Ltd., KENCHIKU GIZYUTSU CENTER, J. V.
f. KAJIMA Corporation Co., Ltd., Matsue Doken J. V.
j. INAX Co., Ltd.

a. 津田沼駅北口歩道橋のペーブパターン
b. 千葉県習志野市
c. 習志野市
f. 白井建設，旭窯業商会
g. 渡辺文作
i. せっ器質無釉タイル
j. ダントー㈱

a. TSUDANUMA STATION NORTH EXIT BRIDGE
   PAVEMENT PATTERN
b. Narashino-shi, Chiba
c. Narashino City
f. Shirai Kensetsu Co., Ltd., Asahi Yogyo Corporation
g. Bunsaku Watanabe
i. Stoneware unglazed tile
j. DANTO CORPORATION

a. ラポルテのペーブパターン
b. 兵庫県芦屋市
c. 芦屋市
e. 環境再開発研究所
f. 竹中工務店・大林組・新井組共同企業体，平田
   タイル
g. 吉田フォトスタジオ
i. せっ器質無釉タイル
j. ダントー㈱

a. LA PORTE PAVEMENT PATTERN
b. Ashiya-shi, Hyogo
c. Ashiya City
d. ENVIRONMENT DEVELPMENT RESEARCH INC.
f. Takenaka Koumuten Co., Ltd., Ohbayashi-Gumi
   Co., Ltd., J. V., Arai-gumi Co., Ltd., J. V., Hirata
   Tile Co., Ltd. Hirata Tile Co., Ltd.
i. Stoneware unglazed tile
g. Yoshida Photo Studio
j. DANTO CORPORATION

a. 新宿駅西口歩道のペーブパターン
b. 東京都新宿区
c. 東京都建設局，小田急電鉄，小田急百貨店
d. 大成建設
e. リョーワ工業㈱
f. 大成建設・小田急建設共同企業体
g. 竹林龍三郎
i. 御影石磁器石材（人工御影石）サンセラミカゲ
j. リョーワ工業㈱

a. SHINZYUKU STATION WEST EXIT BRIDGE
   PAVEMENT PATTERN
b. Shinzyuku-ku, Tokyo
c. Tokyo Metoroporis, Odakyu Corporation
d. TAISEI Corporation
e. RYOWA INDUSTRY Co., Ltd.
f. TAISEI Corporation, Odakyu Kensetsu Co., Ltd., J.
   V.
g. Ryuzahuro Takebayashi
i. RYOWA GRANITE (reconstituted garanite) SAN-
   CERAMIKAGE
j. RYOWA INDUSTRY Co., Ltd.

a. 伊勢佐木モール街のペーブパターン
b. 神奈川県横浜市
c. 伊勢佐木 l，2丁目地区商店振興会
d. 竹中工務店
f. 竹中工務店
h. ペーブパターンに変化を持たせ歩きやすく疲れずに
   ショッピングできる雰囲気を演出した。
j. ㈱ＩＮＡＸ

a. ISEZAKI MALL PAVEMENT PATTERN
b. Yokohama-shi, Kanagawa
c. Isesaki-shoten Shinkokai
d. Takenaka Koumuten Co., Ltd.
f. Takenaka Koumuten Co., Ltd.
h. This pavement has a relaxing feel and makes
   shopping fun
j. INAX Co., Ltd.

a. テンマ・ランブリング街路のペーブパターン
b. 愛知県一宮市
c. 一宮市商店街振興組合
d. 犬飼芳夫
e. 杉本庄司，青木慶子
f. 愛知県一宮土木事務所
g. 中部フォトサービス
h. 県道の街路電線埋設工事を期に，官民協力で路
　上機器を隠しコミュニティ街路デザインを試作，これ
　からの電線埋設の方向を示した。
i. ＩＮＡＸ磁器タイル（150角）
j. 綜合デザインセンター

a. TENMA RAMBLING ROAD PAVEMENT PAT-
　TERN
b. Ichinomiya-shi, Aichi
c. Tenma-dori Sancyome Shopping Street
d. Yoshio Inukai
e. Shoji Sugimoto, Keiko Aoki
f. Ichinomiya City Engineering Office
g. Chubu Photo Service
h. This project involved the community in an effort to
　creat a path over old road, and electric wire
i. INAX tile
j. SOGO DESIGN CENTER

a. 八王子ターミナルビル前のペーブパターン
b. 東京都八王子市
c. 八王子市
d. 交通建築設計事務所，JR東日本
e. 飛島建設・大成建設共同企業体
f. 第一タイル建設
g. 千代田
i. せっ器質無釉タイル
j. ダントー㈱

a. HACHIOJI TERMINAL BUILDING PAVEMENT
   PATTERN
b. Hachioji-shi, Tokyo
c. Hachioji City
d. Transport Architects Associates, East Japan Railway Company
e. TOBISHIMA CORPORATION, TAISEI Corporation, J.
   V.
f. Daiichi Tile Kensetsu Co., Ltd.
g. Chiyoda
i. Stoneware unglazed tile
j. DANTO CORPORATION

a. 兼高かおる旅の資料館
b. 兵庫県津名町
c. 兵庫県
d. 昭和設計
f. 淡路土建，森長組，鍋谷清吉商店
g. 吉田フォトスタジオ
i. 磁器質施釉タイル
j. ダントー㈱

a. KAORU KANETAKA TRAVELING ARTICLES
   MUSUEM
b. Tsuna-machi, Hyogo
c. Hyogo Pre.
d. Showa Sekkei Co., Ltd.
f. Awaji Doken, Morinaga-Gumi, Nabetani Seikichi
   shoten
g. Yoshida Photo Studio
i. Porcelain glazed tile
j. DANTO CORPORATION

a. 吉祥寺サンロードのペーブパターン
b. 東京都武蔵野市
c. 吉祥寺サンロード商店街振興会
d. ㈱綜デザイン研究所
e. リョーワ工業㈱
f. 鹿島道路㈱
g. 竹林龍三郎
i. 御影質磁器石材（人工御影石）サンセラミカゲ
j. リョーワ工業㈱

a. SUN-ROAD KICHIZYOJI, PAVEMENT PAT-
   TERN
b. Musashino-shi, Tokyo
c. Kichizyoji Sun-road Shopping Mall
d. SO DESIGN KENKYUZYO Co., Ltd.
e. RYOWA INDUSTRY Co., Ltd.
f. KAJIMA DORO Coporation
g. Ryuzaburo Takebayashi
i. RYOWA GRANITE (reconstituted garanite) SAN-
   CERAMIKAGE
j. RYOWA INDUSTRY Co., Ltd.

a. 仙台一番街のペーブパターン
b. 宮城県仙台市
c. 一番町商店街振興会
d. 高橋志保彦
f. 日本舗道㈱
h. 東北の海，そしてさざ波を表現。人々の活発な流れ
   を暗示している。
j. ㈱ＩＮＡＸ

a. PAVEMENT AT SENDAI ICHIBAN-STREET
b. Sendai-shi, Miyagi
c. Ichiban-cho Shopping Arcade
d. SHIOHIKO TAKAHASHI ARCHITECTS & ASSOCI-
   ATES
f. NIHON HODO Co., Ltd.
h. Tohoku's ocean and rippling waves, as well as the
   activity of the local people, is represented here
j. INAX Co., Ltd.

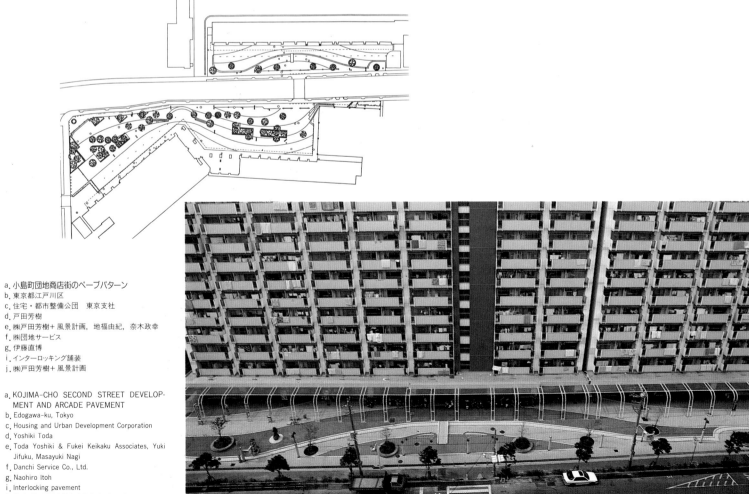

a. 小島町団地商店街のペーブパターン
b. 東京都江戸川区
c. 住宅・都市整備公団　東京支社
d. 戸田芳樹
e. ㈱戸田芳樹＋風景計画，地福由紀，奈木政幸
f. ㈱団地サービス
g. 伊藤直博
i. インターロッキング舗装
j. ㈱戸田芳樹＋風景計画

a. KOJIMA-CHO SECOND STREET DEVELOP-
   MENT AND ARCADE PAVEMENT
b. Edogawa-ku, Tokyo
c. Housing and Urban Development Corporation
d. Yoshiki Toda
e. Toda Yoshiki & Fukei Keikaku Associates, Yuki
   Jifuku, Masayuki Nagi
f. Danchi Service Co., Ltd.
g. Naohiro Itoh
i. Interlocking pavement
j. Toda Yoshiki & Fukei Keikaku Associates

a. 広小路商店街のペーブパターン
b. 愛知県名古屋市
c. 広小路商店街振興会
d. 都市問題研究室
e. リョーワ工業㈱
f. 日米金属建設㈱
g. 竹林龍三郎
i. 御影質磁器石材（人工御影石）サンセラミカゲ
j. リョーワ工業㈱

a. HIROKOJI ARCADE PAVEMENT PATTERN
b. Nagoya-shi, Aichi
c. Hirokoji Shopping Mall
d. Toshi-mondai Kenkyu-shitsu
e. RYOWA INDUSTRY Co., Ltd.
f. Nichibei Kinzoku Kensetsu Co., Ltd.
g. Ryuzaburo Takebayashi
i. RYOWA GRANITE (reconstituted garanite) SAN-CERAMIKAGE
j. RYOWA INDUSTRY Co., Ltd.

a. 玉商店街のペーブパターン
b. 岡山県玉野市
c. 玉商店街振興組合
e. リョーワ工業㈱
f. 鹿島道路㈱
g. 竹林龍三郎
i. 御影質磁器石材（人工御影石）サンセラミカゲ
j. リョーワ工業㈱

a. TAMA SHOPPING MALL PAVEMENT PATTERN
b. Tamano-shi, Okayama
c. Tamano Shopping Mall
e. RYOWA INDUSTRY Co., Ltd.
f. KAJIMA DORO Corporation
g. Ryuzaburo Takebayashi
i. RYOWA GRANITE (reconstituted garanite) SAN-CERAMIKAGE
j. RYOWA INDUSTRY Co., Ltd.

a. 徳山みなみ銀座商店街のペーブパターン
b. 山口県徳山市
c. 徳山みなみ銀座商店街振興組合
d. キジマデザインルーム
e. リョーワ工業㈱
f. 鹿島道路㈱
g. 竹林龍三郎
i. 御影質磁器石材（人工御影石）サンセラミカゲ
j. リョーワ工業㈱

a. TOKUYAMA - MINAMI GINZA SHOPPING
   MALL PAVEMENT PATTERN
b. Tokuyama-shi, Yamaguchi
c. Tokuyama Minami Shopping Mall
d. Kijima Design Room
e. RYOWA INDUSTRY Co., Ltd.
f. KAJIMA DORO Corporation
g. Ryuzaburo Takebayashi
i. RYOWA GRANITE (reconstituted garanite) SAN-
   CERAMIKAGE
j. RYOWA INDUSTRY Co., Ltd.

a. 桜ヶ丘団地のペーブパターン
b. 茨城県水戸市
c. 茨城県土木部住宅課
e. 内井昭蔵建築設計事務所
f. ㈱タカタ
i. 花崗岩
j. ㈱タカタ

a. SAKURAGAOKA HOUSING PROJECTS PAVE-
   MENT PATTERN
b. Mito-shi, Ibaraki
c. Department of Civil Engineering , Ibaraki Pre.
e. S.UCHII ARCHITECTS & ASSOCIATES
f. TAKATA Co., Ltd.
i. Granite
j. TAKATA Co., Ltd.

a. 多摩センター駅前広場のペーブメント
b. 東京都多摩市
c. 住宅・都市整備公団
d. 大高建築設計事務所
h. 幾何学紋様によって遠近法的な空間の奥行を演出した。
j. ㈱INAX

a. TAMA CENTER STATION FRONT SQUARE PAVEMENT PATTERN
b. Tama-shi, Tokyo
c. Housing & Urban Development Corporation
d. Otaka Architects & Associates
h. A geometric pattern expressing various distances
j. INAX Co., Ltd.

a. 天満屋ハッピータウン西大寺のペーブパターン
b. 岡山県岡山市
c. 天満屋
e. 竹中工務店
f. 平松建材
g. 吉田フォトスタジオ
i. せっ器質無釉タイル
j. ダントー㈱

a. TENMAYA HAPPY TOWN SAIDAIJI PAVEMENT PATTERN
b. Okayama-shi, Okayama
c. TENMAYA Corporation
d. Takenaka Koumuten Co., Ltd.
f. Takenaka Koumuten Co., Ltd., Hiramatsu Kenzai Co., Ltd.
g. Yoshida Photo Studio
i. Stoneware unglazed tile
j. DANTO CORPORATION

83

a. 新浦安駅周辺のペーブパターン
b. 千葉県浦安市
c. 浦安市
d. ㈱都市計画設計研究所 河合良樹
e. 郭純、八木健一、加藤秀明
f. 清水建設㈱
h. 色調はブルーグレーとウォームグレー。パターンはグリッド、円形貼りとしている。
i. セラミックタイル／擬石タイル／インターロッキング舗装
j. ㈱八木造景研究所

a. SHIN URAYASU STATION PAVEMENT PAT-TERN
b. Urayasu-shi, Chiba
c. Urayasu City
d. Yoshiki Kawai, Urbanic Planning & Associates
e. Jun kaku, kenichi Yagi, Hideaki kato
f. SHIMIZU CORPORATION
h. In blue grey and warm grey, a circular pattern is expressed
i. Ceramic tile, interrocking pavement
j. YAGI LANDSCAPE DESIGN OFFICE

a. TAS ビルのペーブパターン
b. 山形県長井市
c. 財団法人置賜地域地場産業振興センター，特殊法人山形県信用保証協会，財団法人若者定住促進センター
d. 本間利雄設計事務所＋地域環境計画研究室
e. 本間利雄設計事務所＋地域環境計画研究室，剣持デザイン研究所
f. 清水建設・熊谷組・長井総合建設協同組合共同企業体
g. 菅雅昭
j. 本間利雄設計事務所＋地域環境計画研究室

a. TAS BUILDING PAVEMENT PATTERN
b. Nagai-shi, Yamagata
c. Foundation Oitama Local Area Industrial Promo-tion Center, Nagai Branch of the Yamagata Prefec-ture Credit Guarantee Association, Foundation Center for Promotion of Permanent Residence for Young People
d. Toshio Honmma & Associates
e. Toshio Honmma & Associates
f. SHIMIZU CORPORATION, Kumagai-Gumi Co., Ltd., Nagai General Construction Co-operation, J. V.
g. Masaaki Kan
j. Toshio Honmma & Associates

a. 元町百段公園のペーブメント
b. 神奈川県横浜市
c. 横浜市
d. 戸田芳樹
e. 戸田芳樹＋風景計画，地福由紀，片寄恵
f. 常盤造園㈱
g. 伊藤直博
i. 大谷石／御影石
j. ㈱戸田芳樹＋風景計画

a. MOTOMACHI HYAKUDAN PARK PAVEMENT
   PATTERN
b. Yokohama-shi, Kanagawa
c. Yokohama City
d. Yoshiki Toda
e. Toda Yoshiki & Fukei Keikaku Associates, Yuki
   Jifuku, Megumi Katayose
f. Tokiwa Zoen Co., Ltd.
g. Naohiro Ito
i. Oya stone and granite pavement
j. Toda Yoshiki & Fukei Keikaku Associates

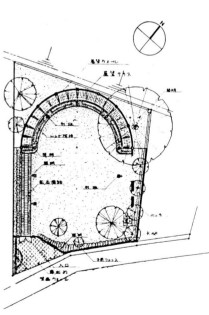

a. 熱海サンビーチ
b. 静岡県熱海市
c. 熱海市観光施設課
d. ㈱ウォーターデザイン
f. 青木建設㈱
h. 円形によって小宇宙を表現するとともに誰にでも親しまれ、愛される広場でありたいと願った。
j. ㈱ウォーターデザイン

a. ATAMI SUN-BEACH PAVEMENT PATTERN
b. Atami-shi, Shizuoka
c. Sightseeing Bureau, Atami City
d. WATER DESIGN Co., Ltd.
f. Aoki Kensetsu Co., Ltd.
h. The circular patterns in this square make it a comfortable, endearing place to one and all
j. WATER DESIGN Co., Ltd.

a. バラ公園のペーブパターン
b. 広島県福山市
c. 福山市
d. 高橋秀幸
f. 藤井タイル
g. 旺映社
i. 磁器質無釉タイル
j. ダントー㈱

a. ROSE PARK PAVEMENT PATTERN
b. Fukuyama-shi, Hiroshima
c. Fukuyama City
d. Hideyuki Takahashi
f. Fujii Tile Co., Ltd.
g. Oei-sha
i. Porcelain unglazed tile
j. DANTO CORPORATION

a. パークシティ新川崎のペーブパターン
b. 神奈川県川崎市
c. 三井不動産㈱
d. 三井不動産㈱，中島幹夫
e. 中島幹夫，都田徹，緒方基秀
f. 鹿島建設㈱，三井建設㈱，長谷製陶
g. 北原美子（北井スタジオ）
h. 住生活者にとって，飽きないホットなデザインを狙った。
i. タイル／インターロック
j. 中島幹夫

a. PARK CITY SHIN-KAWASAKI PAVEMENT PATTERN
b. Kawasaki-shi, Kanagawa
c. Mitsui Real Estate Development, Mikio Nakajima
d. Mikio Nakajima, Mitsui Real Eatate Development
e. Mikio Nakajima, Tooru Miyakoda, Kiyohide Ogata
f. KAJIMA Corporation Co., Ltd., MITSUI KENSETSU Co., Ltd., NAGATANI SEITO Co., Ltd.
g. Yoshiko Kitahara (Kitai Studio)
h. A striking design which the people will not easily tire of
i. Tile, interrock
j. Mikio Nakajima

a. MM21日本丸メモリアルパークのペーブパター
   ン
b. 神奈川県横浜市
c. 横浜市港湾局，㈱みなとみらい２１
d. 三菱地所
e. リョーワ工業㈱
f. 奈良建設㈱
g. 竹林龍三郎
i. 御影質磁器石材（人工御影石）サンセラミカゲ
j. リョーワ工業㈱

a. MM21 NIHONMARU SHIP MEMORIAL PARK
   PAVEMENT PATTERN
b. Yokohama-shi, Kanagawa
c. Minato Mirai 21 Co., Ltd., Yokohama City
d. Mitsubishi Estate Company Limited
e. RYOWA INDUSTRY Co., Ltd.
f. Nara Kensetsu Co., Ltd.
g. Ryuzaburo Takebayashi
i. RYOWA GRANITE (reconstituted granite)
   SANCERAMIKAGE
j. RYOWA INDUSTRY Co., Ltd.

a. MM21日本丸メモリアルパークのペーブパター
   ン
b. 神奈川県横浜市
c. 横浜市港湾局，㈱みなとみらい２１
d. 三菱地所
e. リョーワ工業㈱
f. 奈良建設㈱
g. 竹林龍三郎
i. 御影質磁器石材（人工御影石）サンセラミカゲ
j. リョーワ工業㈱

a. MM21 NIHONMARU SHIP MEMORIAL PARK
   PAVEMENT PATTERN
b. Yokohama-shi, Kanagawa
c. Minato Mirai 21 Co., Ltd., Yokohama City
d. Mitsubishi Estate Company Limited
e. RYOWA INDUSTRY Co., Ltd.
f. Nara Kensetsu Co., Ltd.
g. Ryuzaburo Takebayashi
i. RYOWA GRANITE (reconstituted granite)
   SANCERAMIKAGE
j. RYOWA INDUSTRY Co., Ltd.

a. 神宮パークハイツのペーブパターン
b. 名古屋市
c. 住宅・都市整備公団
f. 平野建材
g. 博英パブリシティ
i. せっ器質無釉タイル
j. ダントー㈱

a. JINGU PARK MANSION PAVEMENT PAT-
  TERN
b. Nagoya-shi, Aichi
c. Housing & Urban Development Corporation
f. Hirano Tile Co., Ltd.
g. HAKUEI Publicity
i. Stoneware unglazed tile
j. DANTO CORPORATION

a. 春日池公園のペーブパターン
b. 広島県福山市
c. 福山市
f. 松原組，野村タイル，藤井タイル
g. 旺映社
i. 磁器質無釉タイル
j. ダントー㈱

a. KASUGA-IKE PARK PAVEMENT PATTERN
b. Fukuyama-shi, Hiroshima
c. Fukuyama City
f. Matsubara-gumi Co., Ltd., Nomura Tile Co., Ltd.,
  Fujii Tile Co., Ltd.
g. Oei-sha
i. Porcelain unglazed tile
j. DANTO CORPORATION

a. 宇都宮市文化会館
b. 栃木県宇都宮市
c. 宇都宮市
e. 佐藤武夫設計事務所
f. 大成建設㈱，不二窯業
g. 渡辺文作
i. せっ器質無釉タイル
j. ダントー㈱

a. UTSUNOMIYA CULTURE HALL PAVEMENT
  PATTERN
b. Utsunomiya-shi, Tochigi
c. Utsunomiya City
d. SATOW ARCHITECTS & ENGINEERS
f. TAISEI Corporation, Fuji Yogyo Co., Ltd.
g. Bunsaku Watanabe
i. Stoneware unglazed tile
j. DANTO CORPORATION

a. 横浜市街路のペーブパターン
b. 神奈川県横浜市
c. 横浜市
e. 八木健一，板垣久美子，長橋義英
h. 緑道整備に伴いゲートからアプローチ部にいたるま
  で色を変化させている。
i. 擬石平板
j. ㈱八木造景研究所

a. YOKOHAMA CITY MALL PAVEMENT PAT-
  TERN
b. Yokohama-shi, Kanagawa
c. Yokohama City
e. Kenichi Yagi, Kumiko Itagaki, Yoshihide Nagahashi.
h. A greenery-rich path of changing color
i. Imitation-stone plat tile
j. YAGI LANDSCAPE DESIGN OFFICE

89

a. グリーンピア津南・中央庭園
b. 新潟県中魚沼郡
c. 年金福祉事業団，(財)年金保養協会
d. ㈱日建設計　森山明
e. 戸田芳樹，地福由紀，藤田和孝，古根聡
f. 西武新潟北越建設工事共同企業体
　　西武新潟グリーン建設工事共同企業体
g. 地福由紀＋藤田和孝
i. 稲田御影石／鉄平石／御影雑割石積／コンクリ
　　ート舗装
j. ㈱戸田芳樹＋風景計画

a. CENTRAL GARDEN, GREEN PIA TSUNAN
b. Nakauonuma-gun, Niigata
c. Annuity Welfare Enterprise, Annuity Recreational Foundation
d. NIKKEN SEKKEI LTD., Akira Moriyama
e. Toda Yoshiki & Fukei Keikaku Associates, Yoshiki Toda, Yuki Jifuku, Kazunori Fujita, Satoshi Furune
f. Seibu, Niigata, Hokuetsu Construction Works J.V. Seibu, Niigata, Green Construction Works J.V.
g. Yuki Jifuku, Kazunori Fujita
i. Inada granite, pulverized granite, concrete paving
j. Toda Yoshiki & Fukei Keikaku Associates

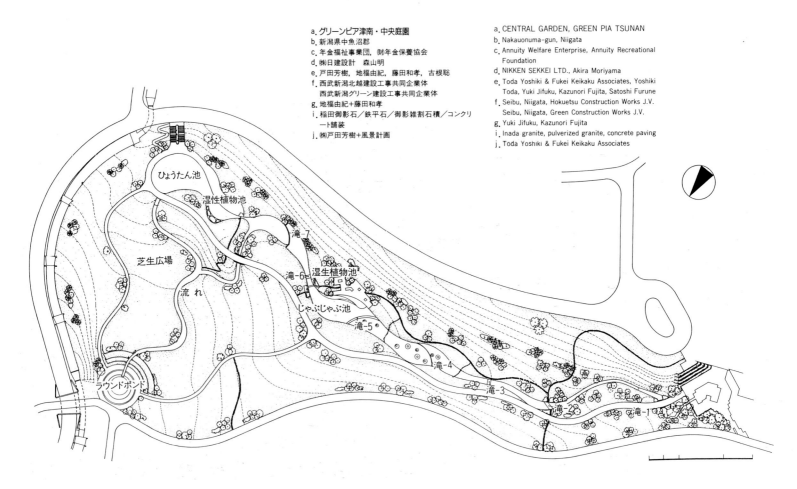

a. 国営海の中道海浜公園・壁泉「飛翔」
b. 福岡県福岡市
c. 建設省九州地方建設局
d. ㈱都市計画研究所
e. 広井力+㈱都市計画研究所
f. 内山緑地建設㈱, ㈱ウォーターデザイン
h. 石彫レリーフと純白な落水のフォルムで, 大地を飛び立つ大鳥の姿をダイナミックに表現した。
i. レリーフ壁=錆御影石（W=32m, H=5m）流水量=毎分15㎥（W=24m）
j. ㈱ウォーターデザイン

a. UMI-NO NAKAMICHI SEASIDE NATIONAL GOVERMENT PARK FOUNTAIN
b. Fukuoka-shi, Fukuoka
c. The Ministry of Construction
d. Toshikeikaku Kenkyujo Co., Ltd.
e. Tsutomu Hiroi
f. Uchiyama Ryokuchi Kensetsu Co., Ltd., WATER DESIGN Co., Ltd.
h. Carved rock and white water create the dynamic form of and a bird taking flight.
i. Relief=granite (W=32m, H=5m), water flow 15m³ per minute
j. WATER DESIGN Co., Ltd.

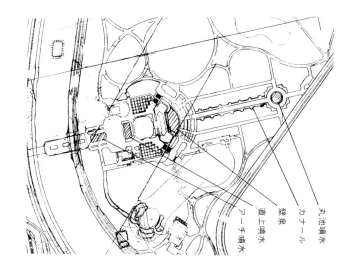

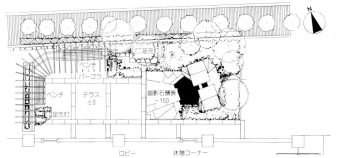

a. 富山県赤坂会館・庭園
b. 東京都港区
c. ㈶富山県赤坂会館
d. 稲垣丈夫
e. 稲垣丈夫, 嶋田博次, 岩村智恵子
f. ㈱川谷内造園
g. ㈱川谷内造園
h. ロビーに接する戸外室として計画し, 急峻な山と岩清水を象徴するモニュメントを中心に構成。
i. 御影石／白御影石／白河石／ナチュラルロックエイト
j. ㈱稲垣ランドスケープデザイン研究所

a. SCULPTURE, TOYAMA PRE・AKASAKA HALL
b. Minato-ku, Tokyo
c. Akasaka Kaikan of Toyama Pre.
d. Takeo Inagaki
e. Takeo Inagaki, Hirotsugu Shimada, Chieko Iwamura
f. Kawayauchi Zoen Co., Ltd.
g. Kawayauchi Zoen Co., Ltd.
h. This lobby was planned as an outdoor room, with a monument symbolizing high mountains and pure water.
i. Granite, white granite (Shirakawa-ishi), river and natural rock
j. Inagaki Landscape Research Institute

a. バーデン市立病院・庭園
b. オーストリア　バーデン市
c. バーデン市
d. マティアス・ヒッツ
e. リンダブルン国際彫刻シンポジウム，横沢英一，高間治彦
f. リンダブルン国際彫刻シンポジウム
g. 片桐宏典
h. 患者，医師，見舞い客などのコミュニケーションの場として，清潔さと楽しさを演出した。
i. れき岩／花崗岩／木
j. ㈱ランドスケープ デザイン コンサルタント

a. BADEN MUNICIPAL CITY HOSPITAL AND GARDEN
b. Baden City, Austoria
c. Baden City
d. Mathias Hietz
e. Rindabrunn International Sculpture Symposium, Hidekazu Yokozawa, Haruhiko Takama
f. Rindabrunn International Sculpture Symposium
g. Hironori Katagiri
h. As a place where patients, doctors and visitors can communicate, this area offers a clean and pleasant atmosphere.
i. Conglomerate, granite and wood
j. LANDSCAPE DESIGN CONSULTANTS Co., Ltd.

a. 東海岸グリーンベルト・噴水
b. 静岡県熱海市
c. 熱海市
e. 富田真平＋㈱ウオーターデザイン
f. ㈱ウォーターデザイン
h. 魅力ある熱海海岸復活を期し、サン・ビーチ計画に
　先駆け、憩いの場として石彫刻「こぶし」と「ささ
　やき」を囲む一対の噴水を設置した。
i. 白御影石
j. ㈱ウォーターデザイン

a. HIGASHI-KAIGAN GREEN BELT FOUNTAIN
b. Atami-shi, Shizuoka
c. Atami City
e. Shinpei Tomita, WATER DESIGN Co., Ltd.
f. WATER DESIGN Co., Ltd.
h. The revival of the charming Atami coastline includ-
　ed the addition of a sand seashore and this rest
　area, with a fountain created form a carved fist,
　which communicates the idea of whispering.
i. White granite
j. WATER DESIGN Co., Ltd.

a.「虹の広場」
b. 東京都江戸川区
c. ㈶江戸川区環境促進事業団
d. ㈱日建設計　森山明
e. 戸田芳樹，島川清史，地福由紀，奈木政幸，伊藤直博，石井英美，村岡将
f. ㈱鹿野建設
g. 伊藤直博
i. 御影小舗石舗装／ステンレスパイプ
j. ㈱戸田芳樹+風景計画

a. RAINBOW SQUARE
b. Edogawa-ku, Tokyo
c. Edogawa-ku, Environmental Enterprise Foundation
d. NIKKEN SEKKEI Ltd., Akira Moriyama
e. Toda Yoshiki & Fukei Keikaku Associates, Yoshiki Toda, Yuki Jifuku, Kiyoshi Shimakawa, Masayuki Nagi, Naohiro Ito, Hidemi Ishii, Masashi Muraoka
f. Shikano Construction Co., Ltd.
g. Naohiro Itoh
i. Granite paving and stainless pipe
j. Toda Yoshiki & Fukei Keikaku Associates

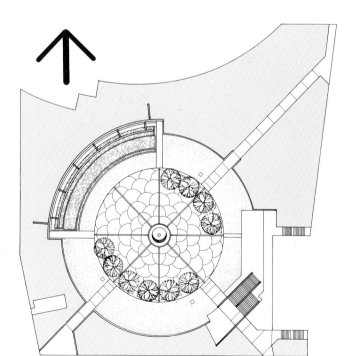

A-A′ 断面図　S=1:50

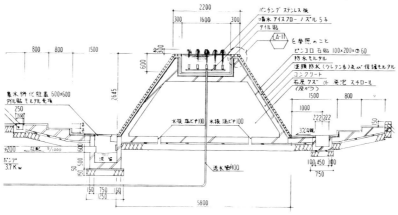

a. 沼津学園高校キャンパス・噴水
b. 静岡県沼津市
c. 沼津学園高校　是村恵三
d. 鹿島建設横浜支店　上法武文
e. 都田徹，横田博，鍛治貴夫，景観設計研究所
f. 鹿島建設，東建工業，アズミック，久保田鉄工
g. 広田治雄，都田徹
h. 富士山の麓に高校生活の若さとみずみずしさ，キャンパス生活の思い出と富士山を象徴する噴水。
i. レンガロック／ピンコロ／リョウワタイル
j. ㈱景観設計研究所東京事務所

a. NUMAZU GAKUEN HIGH SCHOOL CAMPUS FOUNTAIN
b. Numazu-shi, Shizuoka
c. Keizo Koremura, (Numazu Gakuen High School)
d. KAJIMA Corporation Co., Ltd., Takefumi Jōho
e. Total Environmental Design Office, Tokyo., Tooru Miyakoda, Hiroshi Yokota, Takao Kaji
f. KAJIMA, TOKEN KOGYO, AZUMIKKU, KUBOTA TEKKO etc.
g. Haruo Hirota, Tooru Miyakoda
h. The design of this fountain symbolizes Mt. Fuji and the youthful out look of the high school political organization.
i. Brick, tile and pincolo
j. Total Environmental Design Office, Tokyo

a. 美術館壁泉「水舞台」
b. 京都世田谷区
c. 田谷区
d. 関根伸夫＋環境美術研究所
e. 内井昭蔵建築設計事務所
f. ㈱タカタ／千歳金属
g. 広田治雄
h. 壁泉彫刻は入口広場から中庭に下りる階段の落
　差を空間演出の要素に取り入れている。
i. 白御影石（稲田石）／ステンレス
j. 環境美術研究所

a. GATE OF LANDSCAPE & STAGE OF WATER
b. Setagaya-ku, Tokyo
c. Setagaya Ward
d. Nobuo Sekine & Environment Art Studio
e. S. UCHII ARCHITECTS & ASSOCIATES
f. TAKATA Co., Ltd., Chitose Kinzoku
g. Haruo Hirota
h. The spring in the wall incorporates the descent of
　steps from the square down into the garden.
i. White granite, stainless steel
j. Environment Art Studio.

a. ライブタウン綱島・噴水広場
b. 神奈川県横浜市
c. 小山ドライビングスクール綱島
d. 高瀬昭男
e. 高瀬昭男
f. 鹿島建設㈱
g. 紀善久
i. 御影石（サビ、蛭川産）
j. ㈱空間造形研究所

a. FOUNTAIN SQUARE, LIVE TOWN TSUNA-SHIMA
b. Yokohama-shi, Kanagawa
c. Koyama Driving School of Tsunasima
d. Akio Takase
e. Akio Takase
f. KAJIMA Corporation
g. Yoshihisa Kino
h. Granite
i. Urban Space Art Studio Inc.

a. 浜大津西交通広場・噴水「希望の泉」
b. 滋賀県大津市
c. 大津市
d. ㈱都市計画研究所　武本幸治
e. 田村了一、住谷正己
f. ㈱ウォーターデザイン
h. 湖都大津の表玄関、琵琶湖観光の拠点の新たな
　 シンボルとして斬新で軽快な金属フォルムを主体に
　 した。
i. ステンレス／御影石
j. ㈱ウォーターデザイン

a. HAMAOHTSU WEST INTERSECTION
　 FOUTAIN SQUARE
b. Ohtsu-shi, Shiga
c. Ohtsu City
d. Toshikeikaku Kenkyujo Co., Ltd., Koji Takemoto
e. Ryoichi Tamura, Masami Sumiya
f. WATER DESIGN Co., Ltd.
h. The front gate to the park offers a symbol of
　 lightness and metallic form for visitors to Lake
　 Biwako.
i. White granite, stainless
j. WATER DESIGN Co., Ltd.

a. 福岡南公園・壁泉
b. 福岡県福岡市
c. 福岡市
d. 土屋勉
e. ㈱アーバン デザイン コンサルタント
f. ㈱ウォーターデザイン
i. 壁部—六方石木口／木端積み
j. ㈱ウォーターデザイン

a. WALL AND FOUNTAIN
b. Fukuoka-shi, Fukuoka
c. Fukuoka City
d. Tsutomu Tsuchiya
e. URBAN DESIGN CONSULTANTS INC.
f. WATER DESIGN Co., Ltd.
j. WATER DESIGN Co., Ltd.

a. 山梨医科大学・中庭広場
b. 山梨県中巨摩郡
c. 文部省
d. ㈱日本技術開発　田村利久
e. ㈱戸田芳樹風景計画，戸田芳樹，島川清史，吉村ゆみ
f. 富士緑化㈱
g. 伊藤直博
i. レンガタイル舗装／大谷石舗装／コンクリート側壁吹き付け
j. ㈱戸田芳樹＋風景計画

a. YAMANASHI MEDICAL UNIVERSITY, CENTRAL SQUARE GARDEN
b. Nakakoma-gun, Yamanashi
c. The Ministry of Education
d. Japan Technical Development Co., Ltd., Rikyu Tamura
e. Toda Yoshiki & Fukei Keikaku Associates, Yoshiki Toda, Kiyoshi Shimakawa, Yumi Yoshimura
f. Fuji Ryokuka Co., Ltd.
g. Naohiro Itoh
i. Valley rock and brick tile paving, concrete wall
j. Toda Yoshiki & Fukei Keikaku Associates

a. 佐野市民プール
b. 栃木県佐野市運動公園
c. 住宅・都市整備公団
d. 大間武
e. 塩原孝英，戸谷彰夫
g. 大間武
h. のびのびした景観の中でスポーツ，水遊び，トレーニングができる親しみやすいプールとした。
i. プールはRCづくりESづくりとし，プールサイドはインターロッキング，透水性平板とした。
j. ㈱住環境設計

a. SANO PUBLIC POOL
b. Sano-shi, Tochigi
c. Housing and Urban Development Corporation
d. Takeshi Ohma
e. Takahide Shiohara, Akio Toya
g. Takeshi Ohma
h. This popular pool is situated in a refreshing space that affords various training and play facilities.
i. The poolside is interlocking, the pool of RC and ES construction
j. Living Environment Planners Co., Ltd.

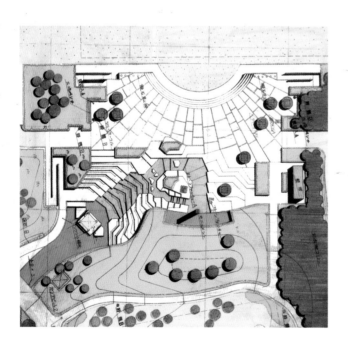

a. 平和の森公園・モニュメント
b. 東京都大田区
c. 大田区
d. 大間武
e. 関根伸夫
g. 大間武
h. 区民が助け合い，協力し合いながら平和な未来社
　会を築く姿を表現する。
i. 白御影石
j. ㈱住環境設計

a. MONUMENT IN "HEIWA-NO MORI" PARK
b. Ohta-ku, Tokyo
c. Ohta-ku
d. Takeshi Ohma
e. Nobuo Sekine
g. Takeshi Ohma
h. The people come together here, in cooperation
　which symbolizes peace in the future.
i. White granite
j. Living Environment Planners Co., Ltd.

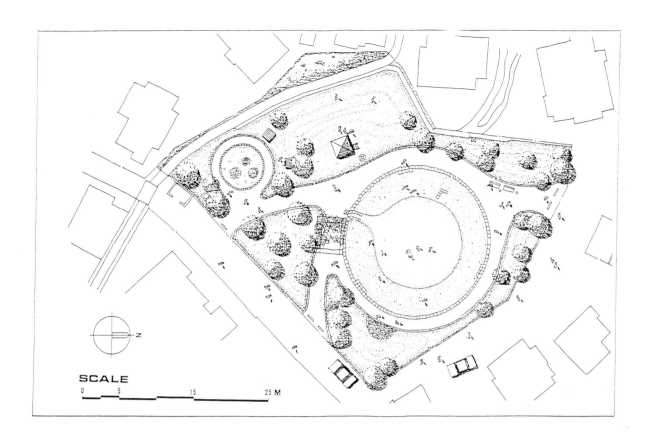

SCALE
0   5   15   25 M

a. 泉町弁天池児童遊園
b. 東京都八王子市
c. 八王子市
d. 栗原国男
e. 藤原清, 栗原国男
f. 東光園緑化㈱
g. 栗原国男
h. 公園中央に湧水を利用した池を配置し, 親水性の
   ある公園として市民に親しまれている。
i. 湧水／安山岩／豆砂利／花／ケヤキ／ハナミズキ
j. ㈱あい造園設計事務所

a. IZUMI-MACHI BENTEN POND CHILDREN'S
   PARK
b. Hachioji-shi, Tokyo
c. Hachioji City
d. Kunio Kurihara
e. Kiyoshi Fujiwara, Kunio Kurihara
f. Tokoen Co., Ltd.
g. Kunio Kurihara
h. A park built around a pond which is formed by
   spring water. A popular place in this town.
j. Ai Landscape Planning Co., Ltd.

a. 噴水モニュメント
b. 千葉県千葉市
c. 住宅・都市整備公団首都圏都市開発本部
e. ライフ計画
f. ㈱サカエ
g. ㈱サカエ 藤田雄次
i. ステンレス／黒御影石
j. ㈱サカエ

a. 錦糸公園・噴水
b. 東京都墨田区
c. 墨田区
d. 大間武
e. 塩原孝英
f. 栗田工業㈱
g. 近藤寛
h. モニュメントと一体となり四季のうつろいを表現した
   噴水は新しい錦糸町のシンボルとなっている。
i. モニュメントはステンレス、噴水池はRCづくりで人
   研、ペイント仕上げとした
j. ㈱住環境設計

a. KINSHI-CHO PARK FOUNTAIN
b. Sumida-ku, Tokyo
c. Sumida Ward Office
d. Takeshi Ohma
e. Takehide Shiohara
f. Kurita Industries Co., Ltd.
g. Hiroshi Kondoh
h. The foutain and the changing seasons are reflected in this monument, a new symbol in Kinshi
   -cho.
j. Living Environment Planners Co., Ltd.

a. 噴水モニュメント
b. 千葉県千葉市
c. 住宅・都市整備公団首都圏都市開発本部
e. ライフ計画
f. ㈱サカエ
g. ㈱サカエ 藤田雄次
i. ステンレス／黒御影石
j. ㈱サカエ

a. FOUNTAIN MONUMENT
b. Chiba-shi, Chiba
c. Housing and Urban Development Corporation
e. Life Landscape Planning Co., Ltd.
f. SAKAE Co., Ltd.
g. Yuji Fujita (SAKAE Co., Ltd.)
i. Stainless steel, black granite
j. SAKAE Co., Ltd.

a. 平和の森公園・パーゴラ
b. 東京都大田区
c. 大田区
d. 大間武
e. 近藤寛
f. ㈱伊藤建設
g. 大間武
h. 白い水平ラインを強調したデザインとし，利用者に
　緑と水に囲まれた憩いの場を提供する。
i. 柱は磁器質タイル貼／パーゴラはスチール製／ペ
　イント仕上げ
j. ㈱住環境設計

a. THE "HEIWA-NO MORI" PARK PERGOLA
b. Ohta-ku, Tokyo
c. Ohta Ward
d. Takeshi Ohma
e. Hiroshi Kondoh
f. Itoh Kensetsu Co., Ltd.
g. Takeshi Ohma
h. The design revolves around the line of the water.
　People rest in surroundings of greenery and water.
i. Columns covered in porcelain tile, steel construc-
　tion
j. Living Environment Planners

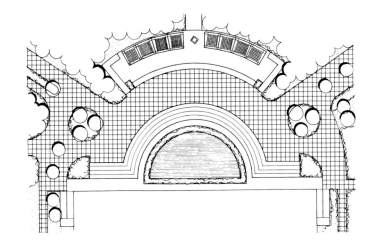

a. TASビルのパーゴラとシェルター
b. 山形県長井市
c. 財置賜地域地場産業振興センター, 特殊法人山形県信用保証協会, 財若者定住促進センター
d. 本間利雄設計事務所+地域環境計画研究室
e. 本間利雄設計事務所+地域環境計画研究室, サイン／剣持デザイン研究所
f. 清水建設, 熊谷組, 長井総合建設協同組合共同企業体
g. 菅雅昭
j. 本間利雄設計事務所+地域環境計画研究室

a. THE TAS BUILDING PERGOLA AND SHELTER
b. Nagai-shi, Yamagata
c. Foundation Oitama Local Area Industrial Promotion Center, Nagai Branch of the Yamagata Prefecture Credit Guarantee Association, Foundation Center for Promotion of Permanent Residence for Young People
d. Toshio Honmma & Associates
e. Toshio Honmma & Associates Associates
f. SHIMIZU CORPORATION, Kumagai-Gumi Co., Ltd. & Nagai General Construction Co-operation, J. V.
g. Masaaki Kan
j. Toshio Homma & Associates

a. 戸塚駅前・バスシェルター
b. 神奈川県横浜市
c. 横浜市都市計画局
d. ㈱GK設計
e. 森田昌嗣，中井川正道
f. ヤマクニ㈱
g. 中佐写真事務所
h. 柱の重い材料と屋根の軽い材料をバランスよく組み
　合せ利用者が気持よく使える構成をめざした。
i. PCコンクリート／ステンレスパイプ／アルミ板
j. ㈱GK設計

a. BAS SHELTER IN TOTSUKA STATION
b. Yokohama-shi, Kanagawa
c. Yokohama City
d. GK Sekkei Associates
e. Yoshitsugu Morita, Masamichi Nakaigawa
f. Yamakuni Co., Ltd.
g. T. NACÁSA & PARTNERS
h. The thoughtful combination of solid pillars and
　light roof material is appreciated by the user.
i. PC concrete, stainless pipe, alminum plate
j. GK Sekkei Associates

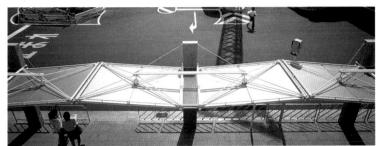

a. 萩指月西公園パーゴラ
b. 山口県萩市
c. 萩市
d. 萩市都市計画課＋横沢英一
e. 横沢英一，高間治彦，田辺武，高間譲治，内藤
　文男，藤本春紀
f. 萩国際彫刻シンポジウム参加者
g. 横沢英一
h. 都市公園の主要な施設を国際彫刻シンポジウムに
　参加した彫刻家達で制作した。
i. 花崗岩（徳山御影石）
j. ㈱ランドスケープ デザイン コンサルタント

a. HAGI SHIZUKI NISHI PARK PERGOLA
b. Hagi-shi, Yamaguchi
c. Hagi City
d. Hagi City Planning Section, Hidekazu Yokozawa
e. Hidekazu Yokozawa, Haruhiko Takama, Takeshi
　Tanabe, Zyouji Takama, Fumio Naitoh, Haruki
　Fujimoto
f. Hagi International Sculpture Symposium
g. Hidekazu Yokozawa
h. On this major facility of the city park sculptors
　from an international symposium participated.
i. Granite
j. Landscape Design Consultant Co., Ltd.

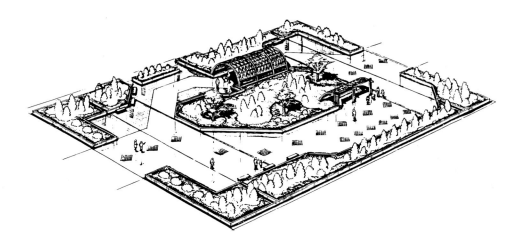

a. 東白鬚公園橋上のパーゴラ
b. 東京都江東区
c. 東京都
d. 東京都第一再開発事務所
e. 大塚正治
f. 京急緑化建設㈱
g. 島田昭治
h. 公園と公園を結ぶ橋上公園に、背景の四角な建物とは対照的な半円柱のウッドパーゴラを設けた。
i. 木材（レッドウッド）
j. ㈱創研

a. "HIGASHI SHIRAHIGE" PARK'S PERGOLA ON THE BRIDGE
b. Koto-ku, Tokyo
c. Tokyo Metropolis
d. Tokyo Metropolis
e. Shoji Otsuka
f. Keikyu Ryokka Construction Co., Ltd.
g. Shoji Shimada
h. For this "park between parks" a half circle,design, in opposition to the square structures surrounding it, was created.
i. Redwood
j. SOUKEN Co., Ltd.

a. 水上パーゴラ
b. 千葉県浦安市しおかぜ緑道
c. 浦安市
d. 村井寿夫
e. 村井寿夫，原貴仁，亀貝絃一郎
f. 三井物産林業㈱
g. 原貴仁
h. 緑陰の少ない明るい緑道の中に、太い木材による日陰と水による涼感の演出を計った。
i. 米ツガ
j. ㈱あい造園設計事務所

a. PERGOLA OVER THE STREAM
b. Urayasu-shi, Chiba
c. Urayasu City
d. Hisao Murai
e. Hisao Murai, Takahito Hara, Koichiro Kamegai
f. Mitsui Bussan Ringyo Co., Ltd.
g. Takahito Hara
h. In this area of little shade, pillars were combined with water to create a refreshing feel.
i. Hemlock spruce
j. Ai Landscape Planning Co., Ltd.

a. パーゴラ
b. 神奈川県横須賀市
c. 神奈川県
d. ㈱都市計画研究所
e. 樋口政善
g. 島田昭治
i. 特殊防腐処理されたダグラスモミ材
j. ㈱創研

a. PERGOLA
b. Yokosuka-shi, Kanagawa
c. Kanagawa Pre.
d. Toshikeikaku Kenkyujo Co., Ltd.
e. Masayoshi Higuchi
g. Shoji Simada
i. Treated Douglas fir
j. SOUKEN Co., Ltd.

a. トライアングル・シェルター
b. 埼玉県岩槻市岩槻公園
c. 岩槻市
d. 平松清房
e. 原貴仁
g. 原貴仁
h. 風景をシェルターにうつし込ませて、建物を消してしまい、風景と建物との同化を計る。
i. ステンレス
j. ㈱あい造園設計事務所

a. TRIANGLE SHELTER
b. Iwatsuki-shi, Saitama
c. Iwatsuki City
d. Kiyofusa Hiramatsu
e. Takahito Hara
g. Takahito Hara
h. Here the scenery is brought into the shelter, eliminating the feeling of a structure and uniting it with the environment.
i. Stainless
j. Ai Landscape Planning Co., Ltd.

a. パーゴラ
b. 愛知県豊田市
c. 豊田市
e. 宮武美弘
f. 内田工業㈱
h. 現代建築風。屋根部にはスモークの入った透明材を使用し、屋根の下でも十分な明るさを保つ。
i. タイル／鋼材／米松／ポリカーボネイト樹脂材
j. 内田工業㈱

a. PERGOLA
b. Toyota-shi, Aichi
c. Toyota City
e. Yoshihiro Miyatake
f. UCHIDA INDUSTRIAL Co., Ltd.
h. An example of modern design. The translucent, smoked roof material allows plenty of light to filter through.
i. Tile, metal, Douglas fir, and polycarbonate laminates.
j. UCHIDA INDUSTRIAL Co., Ltd.

a. パーゴラ
b. 三重県四日市市
c. 四日市市
d. 秋田守人
e. 小久保裕生
f. 内田工業㈱
h. 和風屋根を組み合せたパーゴラ。支柱構造材は鋼管で持たせ、木材の化粧をほどこした。
i. 米松／鋼材／シングル葺
j. 内田工業㈱

a. PERGOLA
b. Yokkaichi-shi, Mie
c. Yokkaichi City
d. Morihito Akita
e. Hiroo Kokubo
f. UCHIDA INDUSTRIAL Co., Ltd.
h. A pergola with a Japanese-style roof. The main support is steel covered with wood.
i. Douglas fir, steel, shingles
j. UCHIDA INDUSTRIAL Co., Ltd.

a. パーゴラ
b. 愛知県名古屋市
c. 名古屋港管理組合
e. 宮武美弘
f. 内田工業㈱
h. 波にうつる太陽と打ち上げられる白い泡をイメージ
   化し、港を訪れる人にやすらぎの空間を与えようと
   試みた。
i. 花崗岩／ステンレス材／米松／ポリカーボネイト樹
   脂材
j. 内田工業㈱

a. PERGOLA
b. Nagoya-shi, Aichi
c. Nagoya Port Administration
e. Yoshihiro Miyatake
f. UCHIDA INDUSTRIAL Co., Ltd.
h. An image similar to that of the sun on the oceans
   bubbling waves. Visitors to the park feel at peace.
i. Granite, stainless materials, Douglas fir, and
   polycarbonate
j. UCHIDA INDUSTRIAL Co., Ltd.

a. 四阿とファニチュア
b. 東京都三鷹市
c. 三鷹市
d. 三鷹市建設部
e. 川口幸雄
g. 島田昭治
h. 緑道にほどよく中の島が設けられており、散策途中
   のひと休み、語らいのレストコーナーになっている。
i. 屋根はアスファルトシングル／柱はダグラスモミ材／
   くずかごはレッドウッド材
j. ㈱創研

a. ARBOR & FURNITURE
b. Mitaka-shi, Tokyo
c. Mitaka City
d. Department of Construction, Mitaka City
g. Shoji Shimada
h. An island where those who are strolling can stop
   for a rest or a chat.
i. Asphalt single roof, Douglas fir pillar and redwood
   trash cans
j. SOUKEN Co., Ltd.

113

a. 置塩邸のパーゴラ
b. 兵庫県宝塚市
c. 置塩郁三
d. 出江寛建築事務所
e. 出江寛
f. シバタ建設工業㈱
g. スタジオ・村井
h. 広大な屋敷に点在する親族の家と自宅へのアプロ
　ーチとして設けられたパーゴラ。
i. 木製 OP／ノーゼンカヅラ
j. 出江寛建築事務所

a. PERGOLA, ORISHIO HOUSE
b. Takarazuka-shi, Hyngo
c. Kunizo Orishio
d. Kan Izue Architects & Associates
e. Kan Izue
f. Shibata Kensetsu Kogyo Co., Ltd.
g. Studio Murai
h. This pergola stands at the approach to residences
　scattered around the large mansion. The resi-
　dences belong to relatives of the owner.
i. Katsura wood
j. Kan Izue Architects & Associates

a. パーゴラ
b. 山梨県石和町
c. 日本道路公団
d. 東京道路エンジニア㈱
g. 島田昭治
i. 特殊防腐処理されたダグラスモミ材
j. ㈱創研

a. PERGOLA
b. Isawa-machi, Yamanashi
c. Japan Road Corporation
d. Tokyo Road Engineer Co., Ltd.
e. Tokyo Road Engineer Co., Ltd.
g. Shoji Shimada
i. Rot-resistant Douglas fir
j. SOUKEN Co., Ltd.

a. 四阿
b. 千葉県銚子市
c. 銚子市
d. 銚子市都市計画課
e. 島田昭治
f. ㈱創研
g. 島田昭治
h. 従来のクローズドな四阿を一変し，天井を吹き抜けにして，モダーンな明るい公園にマッチさせてデザインした。
i. 屋根はアスファルトシングル材/柱とベンチはダグラスモミ材
j. ㈱創研

a. ARBOR
b. Choshi-shi, Chiba
c. Choshi City
d. Town Planning Section, Choshi City
e. Shoji Shimada
f. SOUKEN Co., Ltd.
g. Shoji Shimada
h. Unlike other arbors, this one is designed with an open roof, to blend with the modern and bright park surroundings.
i. Asphalt single roof, bench and beams Douglas fir
j. SOUKEN Co., Ltd.

a. 四阿
b. 埼玉県騎西町
c. 騎西町
d. パシフィックコンサルタント
e. 平井茂俊
f. ㈱創研
g. 佐藤幸雄
h. 従来の四阿とは違う公園用として解放感のある現代風なデザインとした。
i. 屋根は銅板の一文字張り/柱はダグラスモミ材のナグリ仕上げ
j. ㈱創研

a. ARBOR
b. Kisai-machi, Saitama
c. Kisai
d. Pacific Consultants Co., Ltd.
e. Shigetoshi Hirai
f. SOUKEN Co., Ltd.
g. Yukio Sato
h. This arbor differs from past models. It is designed to fit the modern, open style park.
i. The roof is straight copper plate, the construction Douglas fir.
j. SOUKEN Co., Ltd.

a. 四阿
b. 愛知県名古屋市
c. 名古屋市
d. 小笠原弘人
e. 黒野誠一
f. 内田工業㈱
h. 中国風にデザインした。
i. 鋼材/耐候性集成材/花崗岩/銅板
j. 内田工業㈱

a. ARBOR
b. Nagoya-shi, Aichi
c. Nagoya city
d. Hiroto Ogasawara
e. Seiichi Kurono
f. UCHIDA INDUSTRIAL Co., Ltd.
h. A Chinese style design.
i. Reinforcement, climate-resistant conglomerates, stone, copper plate
j. UCHIDA INDUSTRIAL Co., Ltd.

a. 琉球大学医学部のパーゴラ
b. 沖縄県那覇市
c. 文部省
d. 日本技術開発㈱
e. 田村利久
f. 大成道路㈱，㈱仲吉組
g. 島田昭治
h. 堅い感じの建造物と柔らかい感じの庭園の間をつなぎ，日差しや小雨を防ぐ二重構造のパーゴラ。
i. 木材（レッドウッド）
j. ㈱創研

a. RYUKYU UNIVERSITY PERGOLA
b. Naha-shi, Okinawa
c. The Department of Education
d. JAPAN ENGINEERING CONSULTANTS Co., Ltd.
e. Rikyu Tamura
f. Taisei Road Co., Ltd., Nakayoshi-gumi Co., Ltd.
g. Shoji Shimada
h. Meant to provide a transition between "haed" edifices and the garden, this pergola is constructed to provide shelter from rain and sunlight.
i. Redwood
j. SOUKEN Co., Ltd.

a. 琉球大学医学部のパーゴラ
b. 沖縄県那覇市
c. 文部省
d. 日本技術開発㈱
e. 田村利久
f. 大成道路㈱，㈱仲吉組
g. 島田昭治
h. 堅い感じの建造物と柔らかい感じの庭園の間をつなぎ，日差しや小雨を防ぐ二重構造のパーゴラ。
i. 木材（レッドウッド）
j. ㈱創研

a. RYUKYU UNIVERSITY PERGOLA
b. Naha-shi, Okinawa
c. The Department of Education
d. JAPAN ENGINEERING CONSULTANTS Co., Ltd.
e. Rikyu Tamura
f. Taisei Road Co., Ltd., Nakayoshi-gumi Co., Ltd.
g. Shoji Shimada
h. Meant to provide a transition between "haed" edifices and the garden, this pergola is constructed to provide shelter from rain and sunlight.
i. Redwood
j. SOUKEN Co., Ltd.

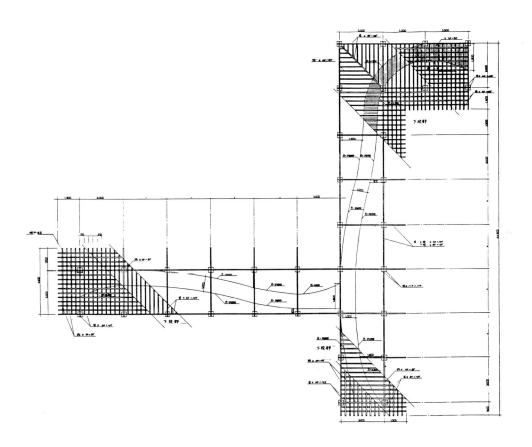

a. 安城駅広場のストリート・ファニュチュア
b. 愛知県安城市
e. 環境開発研究所
g. 仲佐写真事務所
h. 七夕で有名な安城にちなんだデザイン及びマーク
　を入れた備品により楽しい空間を作る。
i. ステンレスにフッ素樹脂塗装仕様。
j. ㈱ダイチ

a. ANJO STATION SQUARE STREET FURNI-
　TURE
b. Anjo-shi, Aichi
e. ENVIRONMENTAL DEVELOPMENT RESEARCH
　INC.
g. T.Nacása & Partners
h. Design marks which explain Anjo's association
　with "Tanabata" enhance the pleasant atmo-
　sphere.
i. Particle board over stainless steel
j. DAICHI Co., Ltd.

a. 大崎駅東口再開発のストリート・ファニチュア
b. 東京都品川区大崎
c. ㈱協立建築設計事務所
g. 仲佐写真事務所
h. 重量感及び高級感のある備品により，うるおいのある公共空間を作り出した。
i. ステンレスと御影石との組み合わせ。
j. ㈱ダイチ

a. STREET FURNITURE IN THE EAST EXIT DEVELOPMENT OF OSAKI STATION
b. Sinagawa-ku, Tokyo
e. KYORITSU ASSOCIATES ARCHITECTS ENGINEERS
g. T.Nacása & Partners
h. The feeling of weight and quality in these articles gives a feeling of opulence.
i. A combination of stainless steel and granite
j. DAICHI Co., Ltd.

a. 侵入禁止ポール
建築物はいつも解放されている。しかし，入れない時間帯もある。シャッターは物理的手段で冷やかに人を阻止する。侵入禁止をヒューマンウエアで発想し視覚的な表現として，この設計となった。

a. スパジオビルのストリートファニチュア
b. 大阪市南区
c. 日進産業株式会社
e. 横田良一，プロダクトデザインルーム　柳澤豊
f. スガツネ工業株式会社
f. 仲佐写真事務所
h. このビルのコンセプトは，建物を単なる器としてではなく都市空間の中の一部として考えフリースルー，フリーインとしてとらえている。ストリートファニチュアについても同じコンセプトを貫いて設計した。

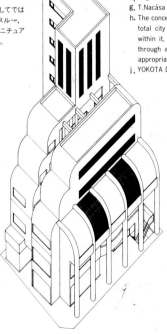

a. SPAZIO (Product)
b. Minami-ku, Osaka-shi
c. Nissin Sangyo Co., Ltd.
e. Ryoichi Yokota, Product Design Room, Yutaka Yanagisawa
f. Sugatsune Kogyo Co., Ltd.
g. T.Nacása & Partners
h. The concept of this building as one element of the total city space, rather than an isolated facility within it, called for the planning of free access through and within. This included the design of appropriate street furniture as well.
j. YOKOTA DESIGN WORK STUDIO INC.

a. 駐車禁止のサイン
法的マークは強制的である。人間的なモラルに訴えるフォルム・ビジュアルによって駐車を遠慮願う意志を表示する。

a. NO PARKING SIGNS
A legal mark is a forceful one. A form that appeals to moral instincts expresses the wish for no parking effectively.

a. AFTER HOURS

Buildings are always open, but there are hours when they are closed to entry. Shutters are psychologically cold and prohibiting, so in this case a more humanistic answer, in visual terms, was built in.

a. ダストボックス
共用スペースに置かれるダストボックスや灰皿は所定の位置に必ずあることが望ましい。美的感覚とクォリティを求め，埋め込み固定した。

a. WASTE BOXE
Waste boxes and ashtrays in public areas should always be placed in set areas. A sense of aesthetic quality is achived by embedding them in certain places.

a. ドアノブ
建築のコンセプトはドアノブにいたるまで美的に表現すべきである。トータルな環境ビジュアルとしてイメージ・コントロールした。

a. DOORKNOBS
The concept of "building" should reach even to doorknobs in the pursuit of quality. This is an element effecting the visual environment.

a. 衆電話ボックス
b. 大建築設計事務所
c. 椎名政夫
j. ㈱ダイチ

a. TELEPHONE BOOTH OF HONDA BUILDING
b. MASAO SHIINA ARCHITECTS
c. MASAO SHIINA
d. DAICHI Co., Ltd.

a. 公衆電話ボックス（新百合ケ丘）
b. 神奈川県川崎市
e. KAN デザイン
j. ㈱ダイチ

a. TELEPHONE BOOTH IN SHIN-YURIGA OKA
b. Kawasaki-shi, Kanagawa
e. KAN DESIGN ASSOCIATES
j. DAICHI Co., Ltd.

a. 俳聖殿ボックス
b. 三重県上野市
c. NTT 上野
e. 中村克久
f. ㈱能登
g. 大村精版印刷
h. 俳聖松尾芭蕉の記念館に設置した。芭蕉が笠と蓑を着た旅姿をイメージしてデザインした。
i. アルミ型材／鉄／ガラス／FRP
j. ㈱能登

a. "HAISEIDEN" TELEPHONE BOOTH
b. Ueno-shi, Mie
c. N.T.T. Ueno
e. Katsuhisa Nakamura
f. Noto Co., Ltd.
g. Omura Printing Co., Ltd.
h. The "Haiseiden" memorial Basyo Matsuo, who wore carried a fulute and wore a "Mino" in his travels, is depicted here.
i. Aluminum, steel, glass, FRP
j. Noto Co., Ltd.

a. 身障者用公衆電話ボックス
b. 富山県高岡市
c. NTT 高岡
e. 上田勉
f. ㈱能登
h. 公共施設には欠かせないボックス。車イスのまま使用できる。外観は切妻屋根と千本格子。
i. アルミ／鉄／ガラス
j. ㈱能登

a. HANDICAPPED PERSONS TELEPHONE BOOTH
b. Takaoka-shi, Toyama
c. N.T.T. Takaoka
e. Tsutomu Ueda
f. Noto Co., Ltd.
h. Designed for use by persons using a wheelchair.
i. Aluminum, steel, glass
j. Noto Co., Ltd.

a. 久喜の公衆電話ボックス
b. 埼玉県久喜市
d. 佐藤武夫設計事務所
g. 仲佐写真事務所
j. ㈱ダイチ

a. TELEPHONE BOOTH IN KUKI
b. Kuki-shi, Saitama
d. SATOW ARCHITECTS & ENGINEERS
g. T.Nacása & Partners
j. DAICHI Co., Ltd.

a. 光が丘の電話ボックス
b. 東京都練馬区
e. スーパーポテト
g. 仲佐写真事務所
j. ㈱ダイチ

a. TELEPHONE BOOTH OF HIKARIGAOKA
b. Nerima-ku, Tokyo
e. Super Potato
g. T. Nacása & Partners
j. DAICHI Co., Ltd.

a. 光が丘の公衆電話ボックス
b. 東京都練馬区
c. ㈱ダイチ
j. ㈱ダイチ

a. TELEPHON BOOTH OF HIKARIGAOKA
b. Nerima-ku, Tokyo
c. DAICHI Co., Ltd.
j. DAICHI Co., Ltd.

a. 救いの電話
b. 福井県坂井郡東尋坊
c. NTT 三国
d. 大沢久広
e. 上田勉
f. ㈱能登
g. 大村精版印刷（合）
h. 自殺の名所東尋坊の「救いの電話」用ボックス。
　　やや離れた所に設置したのが効果が上がっている。
　　ベンチがあるので落ち着く。
i. アルミ／鉄／ガラス／木製ベンチ
j. ㈱能登

a. EMERGENCY TELEPHONE
b. Sakai-gun, Fukui
c. N.T.T.Mikuni
d. Kyuko Osawa
e. Tsutomu Ueda
f. Noto Co., Ltd.
g. Ohmura Printing Co., Ltd.
h. Designed for individuals seeking help in times of
　emotional stress, this effective facility is placed in
　a somewhat isolated area.
i. Aluminum, steel, glass, and wood bench
j. Noto Co., Ltd.

a. 灯台型公衆電話ボックス
b. 千葉県銚子市
c. ㈶電気通信共済会千葉営業所
e. ㈱能登＋NTT 銚子
f. ㈱能登
g. ㈱能登
h. 犬吠埼灯台がある銚子市の環境にふさわしいデザ
　インとした。夜も明るく回りを照らしている。
i. アクリル／ステンレス
j. ㈱能登

a. LIGHT HOUSE STYLE TELEPHONE BOOTH
b. Choshi-shi, Chiba
c. Telwel Chiba
e. Noto Co., Ltd. N.T.T. Choshi
f. Noto Co., Ltd.
h. Designed suitably for Choshi having the Inubosaki
　light house. This telephone booth makes evenings
　bright.
i. Acrylic and stainless
j. Noto Co., Ltd.

a. シティ オブ シモダ
b. 静岡県下田市
c. 下田市役所
d. 鳴瀬秀夫
e. 鳴瀬秀夫
f. ㈱長村製作所
g. 内田フォト
h. 漆喰壁のある街並のイメージを大事にしてデザインした。時計をつけて公共性を配慮した。
i. 漆喰／モルタル／鋼材／ガラス／アルミ
j. ㈱長村製作所

a. TELEPHONE BOOTH, CITY OF SHIMODA
b. Shimoda-shi, Shizuoka
c. Shimoda City
d. Hideo Naruse
e. Hideo Naruse
f. Nagamura Co., Ltd.
g. Uchida Photo
h. This stucco wall, complete with a clock, fits the town image well.
i. Mortar, reinforces, glass, and aluminum
j. Nagamura Co., Ltd.

a. ヨーロピアン・クラシック
b. 神奈川県横浜市
c. NTT
f. ㈱長村製作所
g. 内田フォト
j. ㈱長村製作所

a. EUROPEAN CLASSIC STYLE TELEPHONE BOOTH
b. Yokohama-shi, Kanagawa
c. N.T.T
f. Nagamura Co., Ltd.
g. Uchida Photo
j. Nagamura Co., Ltd.

a. 国技館の公衆電話ボックス
b. 東京都墨田区
c. NTT
d. 鳴瀬秀夫
e. 鳴瀬秀夫
f. ㈱石橋建設
g. 内田フォト
h. 新設の国技館オープンに伴い、国技館をモチーフとしてデザインした。
i. アルミ／強化ガラス／鉄
j. ㈱長村製作所

a. TELEPHONE BOOTH AT THE KOKUGI-KAN
b. Sumida-ku, Tokyo
c. N.T.T.
d. Hideo Naruse
e. Hideo Naruse
f. Ishibashi Kensetsu Co., Ltd.
g. Uchida Photo
h. Designed for the opening of the new gymnasium.
i. Aluminum, reinforced glass, steel
j. Nagamura Co., Ltd.

a. ステンドグラスの公衆電話ボックス
b. 兵庫県芦屋市
c. 芦屋市
f. 東亜通信工材㈱
h. ステンドグラスの屋根はホットとクール，夜は華麗なシルエットを描き街を彩る。
i. カラーアルマイト／ステンドグラス／強化ガラス
j. 東亜通信工材㈱

a. STAINED-GLASS TELEPHONEBOOTH
b. Ashiya-shi, Hyogo
c. Ashiya City
f. Toa-tsushin Kozai Co., Ltd.
h. The stained glass roof creates both a cool and warm feeling, and makes a beautiful silhouette at night
i. Color alumite, stained and reinforced glass
j. Toa-tsushin Kozai Co., Ltd.

a. 中国風公衆電話ボックス
b. 兵庫県神戸市
c. 南京町商店街振興組合
f. 東亜通信工材㈱
h. 中華街にマッチするよう屋根は中国の楼門風，赤と緑の極彩色で仕上げている。
i. スチール焼付塗装／強化ガラス
j. 東亜通信工材㈱

a. CHINESE STYLE TELEPHONEBOOTH
b. Kobe-shi, Hyogo
c. Nankin-machi Shinko Kumiai
f. Toa-tsushin Kozai Co., Ltd.
h. The 'romon' style roof, in bright red and green, is appropriate in this Chinatown setting.
i. Laminated steel and glass
j. Toa-tsushin Kozai Co., Ltd.

a. 立川のガードレール
b. 東京都立川市
e. 永原浄デザイン研究所
g. 仲佐写真事務所
j. ㈱ダイチ

a. FENCE OF TACHIKAWA STATION
b. Tachikawa-shi, Tokyo
e. Jo Nagahara DESIGN ASSOCIATES
g. T. Nacasa & Partners
j. DAICHI Co., Ltd.

a. 蚕糸の森公園の車止め
b. 東京都杉並区
c. 東武緑地建設㈱
d. 杉並区役所
e. 住宅・都市整備公団港北開発局増田元邦
f. 東武緑地建設㈱
h. シンプルで落ち着きのある鋳鉄製。
i. 鋳鉄
j. 第一機材㈱

a. PARKING LOT OF "SANSHI-NO-MORI" FOR-
　　EST PARK
b. Suginami-ku, Tokyo
c. Tobu Ryokuchi Kensetsu Co., Ltd.
d. Suginami Head Office
e. Housing and Urban Development Corporation
f. Tobu Ryokuchi Kensetsu Co., Ltd.
h. Simple and 'relaxed' cast iron.
i. Cast iron.
j. Daiichi Kizai Co., Ltd.

a. 馬事公苑の車止
b. 東京都世田谷区
d. 世田谷区
e. 世田谷区都市デザイン室
g. 仲佐写真事務所
i. 南部鉄
j. ㈱ダイチ

a. PARKING LOT IN BAJIKOEN PARK
b. Setagayaku, Tokyo
d. Setagaya
e. Department of Planning Urban Design Section,
　　Setagaya Ward
g. T. Nacása & partners
i. Nanbu Cast Iron.
j. DAICHI Co., Ltd.

a. 川崎駅のフェンス
b. 神奈川県川崎市
d. ㈱日建設計
e. ㈱日建設計
j. ㈱ダイチ

a. FENCE IN KAWASAKI
b. Kawasaki-shi, Kanagawa
d. NIKKEN SEKKEI LTD.
e. NIKKEN SEKKEI LTD.
j. DAICHI Co., Ltd.

a. パークシティ新川崎のストリート・ファニュチュア
b. 神奈川県川崎市幸区
c. 三井不動産㈱
d. 三井不動産㈱・中島幹夫
e. 都田徹，緒方基秀，飯田清治
f. 鹿島建設㈱，三井建設㈱，㈱創研，関東コンクリート㈱
g. 都田徹／北井スタジオ・北原美子
h. 集合住宅の中で長持ちし，人々に飽きられない親しみやすいものをねらった。
i. 擬石／米松
j. 中島幹夫

a. STREET FURNITURE IN PARK CITY, SHIN-KAWASAKI
b. Kawasaki-shi, Kanagawa
c. Mitsui Real Estate Development
d. Mitsui Real Estate Development, Mikio Nakajima
e. KAJIMA Corporation, Tooru Miyakoda, Motohide Ogata, Seiji Iida
f. KAJIMA Corporation, MITSUI KENSETSU, SOUKEN Co., Ltd., Kanto Concrete
g. Tooru Miyakoda, Yoshiko Kitahara (Kitai-Studio)
h. Durable furniture with appeal was sought for this living development.

i. Molded stone and Douglas fir
j. Mikio Nakajima

a. 親と子のスツール
b. 埼玉県入間市
c. 入間市児童センター
d. 川口寿
e. 柴田さゆり
f. ㈱コトブキ
g. 安藤孝
h. 昔、親から教わった遊びを自分たちの子供にも伝え
　たい。そんな気持ちでデザインした。
i. 磁器
j. ㈱コトブキ

a. PARENT-CHILD STOOL
b. Iruma-shi, Saitama
c. Iruma-shi, Child Center
d. Hisashi Kawaguti
e. Sayuri Shibata
f. KOTOBUKI Co., Ltd.
g. Takashi Ando
h. This was designed to help teach children the game
　their parents played
i. Porcelain
j. KOTOBUKI Co., Ltd.

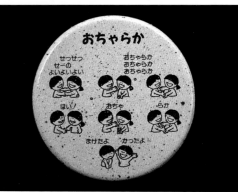

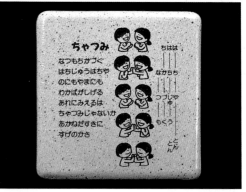

a. 商店街広場のベンチ
b. 東京都世田谷区
c. 住宅・都市整備公団東京支社
d. 戸田芳樹
e. ㈱戸田芳樹＋風景計画／奈木政幸／伊藤直博
f. ㈱団地サービス
g. 伊藤直博
j. ㈱戸田芳樹＋風景計画

a. BENCH
b. Setagaya-ku, Tokyo
c. Housing and Urban Development Corporation
d. Yoshiki Toda
e. Toda Yoshiki & Fukei Keikaku Associates, Masayuki Nagi, Naohiro Itoh
f. Danchi Service Co., Ltd.
g. Naohiro Itoh
j. Toda Yoshiki & Fukei Keikaku Associates

a. 秋穂中学校・石のベンチ
b. 山口県秋穂町
c. 秋穂町
d. 秋穂町企画課
e. 田辺武
f. 田辺武
g. 栗林和彦
i. 花崗岩（秋穂町産）／ステンレスパイプ／芝生
j. 田辺武

a. BENCH IN JR. HIGH SCHOOL
b. Aio-cho, Yamaguchi
c. Aio-cho
d. Planning section of Aio-cho office
e. Takeshi Tanabe
f. Takeshi Tanabe
g. Kazuhiko Kuribayashi
i. Granite, grass, stainless pipe
j. Takeshi Tanabe

a. 商店街のベンチ
b. 横浜市
c. 横浜馬車道商店街
d. 高橋志保彦建築設計事務所
e. 高橋志保彦＋今井庸介
f. ㈱コトブキ
g. 安藤孝
h. 馬をデザインのモチーフに設定，表情のこまやかさ
   を表現するため，黄河の砂を使った鋳物で製作し
   た。
i. 鋳鉄／ナラ材
j. ㈱コトブキ

a. BENCH
b. Yokohama-shi, Kanagawa
c. Bashamichi Shopping Street
d. SHIOHIKO TAKAHASHI & ARCHITECTS & ASSOCI-
   ATES
e. Shiohiko Takahashi, Yosuke Imai
f. Kotobuki Co., Ltd.
g. Takashi Ando
h. In order to create a warm image in this design of
   a horse, sand from Yellow River was used in the
   casting.
i. Cast iron/Nara wood
j. Kotobuki Co., Ltd.

a. 仙台のベンチ
b. 宮城県仙台市
d. 日本舗道㈱
e. 黒瀬歩行
g. 仲佐写真事務所
j. ㈱ダイチ

a. BENCH IN SENDAI STATION
b. Sendai-shi, Miyagi
c. Sendai City
d. NIHON HODO Co., Ltd.
e. Tadayuki Kurose
g. T. Nacàsa & Partners
j. DAICHI Co., Ltd.

a. 川崎駅前のベンチ
b. 神奈川県川崎市
d. ㈱日建設計
e. ㈱日建設計
g. 仲佐写真事務所
j. ㈱ダイチ

a. BENCH IN KAWASAKI STATION
b. Kawasaki-shi, Kanagawa
d. NIKKEN SEKKEI Ltd.
e. NIKKEN SEKKEI Ltd.
g. T. Nacàsa & Partners
j. DAICHI Co., Ltd.

a. 鹿児島美術館のベンチ
b. 鹿児島県鹿児島市
d. ダイチ㈱
g. 仲佐写真事務所
i. 南部鉄
j. ダイチ㈱

a. BENCH IN KAGOSHIMA MUSEUM OF ART
b. Kagoshima-shi, Kagoshima
d. DAICHI Co., Ltd.
g. T. Nacàsa & Partners
i. Granite, Nanbu cast iron
j. DAICHI Co., Ltd.

a. 仙台第一生命ビルのベンチ
b. 宮城県仙台市
e. ダイチ㈱
g. 仲佐写真事務所
j. ㈱ダイチ

a. BENCH IN SENDAI
b. Sendai-shi, Miyagi
d. DAICHI Co., Ltd.
e. DAICHI Co., Ltd.
g. T. Nacàsa & Partners
j. DAICHI Co., Ltd.

a. 所沢のベンチ
b. 埼玉県所沢市
d. U.D.I タカハ都市科学研究所
e. U.D.I タカハ都市科学研究所
g. 仲佐写真事務所
j. ㈱ダイチ

a. BENCH IN TOKOROZAWA STATION
b. Tokorozawa-shi, Saitama
d. URBAN DYNAMIC INSTITUTE OF TAKAHA
e. URBAN DYNAMIC INSTITUTE OF TAKAHA
g. T. Nacàsa & Partners
j. DAICHI Co., Ltd.

a. BYGSビルのベンチ
d. ㈱日建設計
e. ㈱日建設計
g. 仲佐写真事務所
j. ㈱ダイチ

a. BENCH IN BIGS BUILDING
b. Shinzyuku-ku, Tokyo
d. NIKKEN SEKKEI Ltd.
e. NIKKEN SEKKEI Ltd.
g. T. Nacàsa & Partners
j. DAICHI Co., Ltd.

a. 世田谷美術館のベンチ
b. 東京都世田谷区
c. 世田谷区
d. 内井昭蔵建築設計事務所
e. 内井昭蔵建築設計事務所
g. 仲佐写真事務所
j. ㈱ダイチ

a. BENCH IN SETAGAYA MUSEUM OF ART
b. Setagaya-ku, Tokyo
d. S. UCHII ARCHITECTS & ASSOCIATES
e. S. UCHII ASSOCIATES & ASSOCIATES
g. T. Nacàsa & Partners
j. DAICHI Co., Ltd.

a. 暁埠頭公園のベンチ
b. 東京都江東区
c. 東京都
d. 東京都港湾局
e. 大塚正治, 二村絢子
f. 東京園芸㈱
g. 下井三郎
h. 海上公園の芝生広場にどっかりと置かれた風格の
　ある尺角の角材。木彫りで自然との調和を計った
i. レッドウッド/285ミリ角
j. ㈱創研

a. BENCH IN AKATSUKI FUTO PARK
b. Koto-ku, Tokyo
c. Tokyo Metropolis
d. Harbor Department of Tokyo Metropolis
e. Shoji Otsuka, Junko Futamura
f. Tokyo Engei Co., Ltd.
g. Saburo Shimoi
h. Placed in this park on the grass, the square wood
　carving stands as a massive, natural-looking
　marker
i. 285mm california redwood
j. SOUKEN Co., Ltd.

a. 仙台駅前のベンチ
b. 宮城県仙台市
c. 仙台市
d. 日本舗道㈱
e. 黒瀬渉行
g. 仲佐写真事務所
j. タイチ㈱

a. BENCH IN SENDAI STATION
b. Sendai-shi, Miyagi
c. Sendai City
d. NIHON HODO Co., Ltd.
e. Tadayuki Kurose
g. T. Nacàsa Partners
j. DAICHI Co., Ltd.

a. 高輪美術館のベンチ
b. 長野県軽井沢町
c. ㈱西武百貨店
d. アルプ設計室
e. 内藤恒方
f. ㈱西洋環境開発
g. 鹿子丈夫
i. レッドウッド材85角
j. ㈱創研

a. BENCH IN TAKANAWA ART MUSEUM
b. Karuizawa-machi, Nagano
c. Seibu Corporation
d. A. L. P. Designers Inc.
e. Tsunekata Naito
f. Seiyo Kankyo Kaihatsu
g. Takeo Kanoko
i. 85㎜ Square redwood
j. SOUKEN Co., Ltd.

a. 地域センターのベンチ
b. 東京都世田谷区
c. 世田谷区
d. テイクナイン計画設計研究所
e. 中地正隆
g. 島田昭治
i. カルフォルニア・レッドウッド材/134角
j. ㈱創研

a. BENCH
b. Setagaya-ku, Tokyo
c. Setagaya Ward
d. Take 9 Architects Consultants
e. Masataka Nakachi
g. Shoji Shimada
i. California redwood
j. SOUKEN Co., Ltd.

a. 城山公園のベンチ
b. 千葉県館山市
c. 館山市
d. イービーアイ㈱
e. 岡崎章臣
g. 島田昭治
i. カルフォルニア・レッドウッド材
j. ㈱創研

a. BENCH IN SHIROYAMA PARK
b. Tateyama-shi, Chiba
c. Tateyama City
d. Environmental Planning Ins.
e. Akiomi Ōkazaki
g. Shoji Shimada
i. California redwood
j. SOUKEN Co., Ltd.

a. 新百合ケ丘の灰皿とくずかご
b. 神奈川県川崎市
d. KAN デザイン
e. KAN デザイン
g. 仲佐写真事務所
j. ㈱ダイチ

a. ASHTRAY & WASTEBASKET IN YURIGAOKA
b. Kawasaki-shi, Kanagawa
e. KAN DESIGN ASSOCIATES
g. T. Nacàsa & Partners
j. DAICHI Co., Ltd.

a. 国技館の灰皿とくずかご
b. 東京都墨田区
e. ㈱ダイチ
g. 仲佐写真事務所
j. ㈱ダイチ

a. ASHTRAY & WASTEBASKET IN KOKUGI-KAN
b. Sumida-ku, Tokyo
d. DAICHI Co., Ltd.
e. DAICHI Co., Ltd.
g. T. Nacàsa & Partners
j. DAICHI Co., Ltd.

a. 新宿センタービルの灰皿とくずかご
b. 東京都新宿区
d. ㈱ダイチ
e. ㈱ダイチ
g. 仲佐写真事務所
i. ステンレス（鏡面仕上げ）
j. ㈱ダイチ

a. ASHTRAY & WASTEBASKET IN SHINZYUKU
   CENTER BUILDING
b. Shinzyuku-ku, Tokyo
d. DAICHI Co., Ltd.
e. DAICHI Co., Ltd.
g. T.Nacàsa & Partners
i. Stainless
j. DAICHI Co., Ltd.

a. くずかご
b. 埼玉県所沢市
c. ㈱西武百貨店
d. 藤川正夫
e. ㈱乃村工芸社
f. ㈱創研
g. 島田昭治
i. ボックスはレッドウッド材/内かごはステンレス
j. ㈱創研

a. WASTEBASKET
b. Tokorozawa-shi, Saitama
c. Seibu Corporation
d. Masao Fujikawa
e. Nomura Kogei-sha
f. SOUKEN Co., Ltd.
g. Shoji Shimada
i. Redwood, stainless steel
j. SOUKEN Co., Ltd.

a. 新宿グリンタワービルの灰皿とくずかご
b. 東京都新宿区
e. ㈱ダイチ
g. 仲佐写真事務所
i. ステンレス
j. ㈱ダイチ

a. ASHTRAY & WASTEBASKET IN SHINZYUKU GREEN TOWER BUILDING
b. Shinzyuku-ku, Tokyo
e. DAICHI Co., Ltd.
g. T. Nacàsa & Partners
i. Stainless
j. DAICHI Co., Ltd.

a. 広尾ガーデンヒルズの灰皿とくずかご
b. 東京都渋谷区
d. ㈱ダイチ
e. ㈱ダイチ
g. 仲佐写真事務所
j. ㈱ダイチ

a. ASHTRAY & WASTEBASKET IN HIROO GARDEN HILLS BUILDING
b. Shibuya-ku, Tokyo
d. DAICHI Co., Ltd.
e. DAICHI Co., Ltd.
g. T. Nacàsa & Partners
j. DAICHI Co., Ltd.

a. 沖縄熱帯ドリームセンターの灰皿とくずかご
b. 沖縄県沖縄市
d. 日本設計事務所
e. 日本設計事務所
g. 仲佐写真事務所
i. 磁器とステンレス
j. ㈱ダイチ

a. ASHTRAY & WASTEBASKET
b. Okinawa-shi, Okinawa
d. NIHON ARCHITECTS, ENGINEERS & CONSULTANT, INC.
e. NIHON ARCHITECTS, ENGINEERS & CONSULTANT, INC.
g. T. Nacàsa & Partners
i. Ceramic, stainless
j. DAICHI Co., Ltd.

a. 沖縄熱帯ドリームセンターの灰皿とくずかご
b. 沖縄県沖縄市
d. 日本設計事務所
e. 日本設計事務所
g. 仲佐写真事務所
i. 磁器/ステンレス
j. ㈱ダイチ

a. ASHTRAY & WASTEBASKET IN OKINAWA
b. Okinawa-shi, Okinawa
d. NIHON ARCHITECTS, ENGINEERS & CONSUL-
   TANT, INC.
e. NIHON ARCHITECTS, ENGINEERS & CONSUL-
   TANT, INC.
g. T. Nacàsa & Partners
i. Ceramic, stainless
j. DAICHI Co., Ltd.

a. 灰皿とくずかご
b. 山梨県北巨摩郡
c. ㈱創研
d. 佐藤幸雄
e. 下井三郎
g. 深沢寛
i. くずかごはカルフォルニア・レッドウッド材/灰皿は鋳
  物
j. ㈱創研

a. ASHTRAY & WASTEBASKET
b. Kitakoma-gun, Yamanasi
c. SOUKEN Co., Ltd.
d. Yukio Sato
e. Saburo Shimoi
g. Hiroshi Fukazawa
i. California redwood, cast iron, pulverulent painting
j. SOUKEN Co., Ltd.

a. 県立近代美術館の天水鉢
b. 滋賀県大津市
c. 滋賀県
d. 丸伊製陶㈱
e. ㈱日建設計
f. ㈱竹中工務店
g. 間瀬久生
i. 信楽焼
j. 丸伊製陶㈱

a. "TENSUI-BACHI" WATER BALL
b. Ohtsu-shi, Shiga
c. Shiga Pre.
e. NIKKEN SEKKEI Ltd.
f. Takenaka Koumuten Co., Ltd.
g. Hisao Mase
i. Ceramic (Sigaraki-yaki)
j. Marui-seito Co., Ltd.

a. びわこ文化公園のストリートファニチュア
b. 滋賀県大津市
c. 滋賀県
g. 間瀬久生
i. 信楽焼
j. 丸伊製陶㈱

a. STREET FURNITURE IN THE LAKESIDE
   PARK BIWAKO
b. Ohtsu-shi, Shiga
c. Shiga Pre.
g. Hisao Mase
i. Ceramic (Shigaraki-yaki)
j. Marui-seito Co., Ltd.

a. 水飲み
b. 茨城県 つくば市
c. 住宅・都市整備公団
d. 高橋志保彦
e. 高橋志保彦
f. 前田屋外美術㈱
g. 松岡正俊
h. 曲がったスプーンをイメージするこの水飲みは利用者が楽に利用できるようにデザインした。
i. ステンレス
j. ㈱高橋志保彦建築設計事務所

a. DRINKING FOUNTAIN
b. Tsukuba-shi, Ibaraki
c. Housing & Urban Development Corporation
d. Shiohiko Takahashi
e. Shiohiko Takahashi, Masatoshi Matsuoka
f. Maeda Okugai Bizyutsu Co., Ltd.
g. Masatoshi Matsuoka
h. Users enjoy drinking from this fountain, which looks like a bent spoon
i. Stainless
j. SHIOHIKO TAKAHASHI ARCHITECTS & ASSOCIATES

a. 大崎駅東口再開発の水飲み
b. 東京都品川区
d. 協立建築設計事務所
e. 協立建築設計事務所
g. 仲佐写真事務所
j. ㈱ダイチ

a. DRINKING FOUTAIN, OSAKI STATION
b. Shinagawa-ku, Tokyo
d. KYORITSU ASSOCIATES ARCHITECTS ENGINEERS
e. KYORITSU ASSOCIATES ARCHITECTS ENGINEERS
g. T. Nacàsa & Partners
j. Stainless steel
j. DAICHI Co., Ltd.

a. 希望ケ丘商店街の水飲み
b. 東京都世田谷区
c. 住宅・都市整備公団
d. 戸田芳樹
e. ㈱戸田芳樹+風景計画, 奈木政幸, 伊藤直博
f. ㈱団地サービス
g. 伊藤直博
j. ㈱戸田芳樹+風景計画

a. DRINKING FOUNTAIN IN KIBOGAOKA
b. Setagaya-ku, Tokyo
c. Housing & Urban Development Corporation
d. Yoshiki Toda
e. Toda Yoshiki & Fukei Keikaku Associates, Masayuki Nagi, Naohiro Ito
f. Danchi Service Co., Ltd.
g. Naohiro Ito
j. Toda Yoshiki & Fukei Keikaku Associates

a. 水飲み
b. 愛知県長久手町
c. 長久手町
d. 小久保裕生
e. 仲谷直浩
f. 内田工業㈱
g. 松本美智子
h. 水飲みの機能だけでなくモニュメントの役割を果たすよう設計した
i. 大理石
j. 内田工業㈱

a. DRINKING FOUNTAIN
b. Nagakute-machi, Aichi
c. Nagakute
d. Hiroo Kokubo
e. Naohiro Nakaya
f. UCHIDA INDUSTRIAL Co., Ltd.
g. Michiko Matsumoto
h. This is very useful for drinking and monument
i. Granite
j. UCHIDA INDUSTRIAL Co., Ltd.

a. 多摩ニュータウンの歩行者専用路
b. 東京都八王子市
c. 東京都
d. ㈱アーバンデザインコンサルタント
e. ㈱戸田芳樹＋風景計画, 戸田芳樹, 伊藤直博, 奈木政幸
g. 伊藤直博
i. 洗い出し平板舗装
j. ㈱戸田芳樹＋風景計画

a. PEDESTRIAN PATH
b. Hachioji-shi, Tokyo
c. Tokyo Metropolis
d. Urban Design Consultants INC.
e. Toda Yoshiki & Fukei Keikaku Associates, Yoshiki Toda, Naohiro Ito, Masayuki Nagi
g. Naohiro Ito
j. Toda Yoshiki & Fukei Keikaku Associates

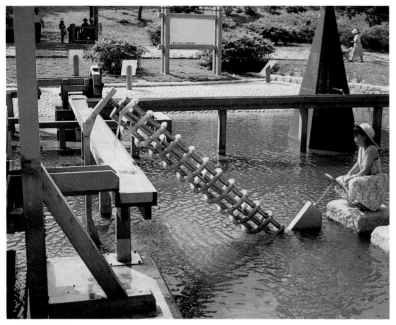

a. おもしろポンド
b. 茨城県十王町
c. 茨城県
d. 茨城県観光課
e. ㈱ブレック研究所
f. ㈱秋山工務店＋㈱三英商会
g. ㈱三英商会　中村明
h. 体験しながら水と親しみ，自然に水の利用法が体
　得できる学習道具として企画した。
i. 米杉／ステンレス
j. ㈱三英商会

a. FUN POND
b. Zyuoh-machi, Ibaraki
c. Ibaraki Pre.
d. Sightseeing Section, Ibaraki Pre.
e. PREC Institute Co., Ltd.
f. AKIYAMA Engineering Co., Ltd., SANEI Co., Ltd.
g. Akira Nakamura, SANEI Co., Ltd.
h. Learning to play with water in a natural way.
i. Douglas fir and stainless steel
j. SANEI Co., Ltd.

a. 湘南海岸公園の帆船滑り台
b. 神奈川県藤沢市
c. 神奈川県湘南海岸整備事務所
d. 三貴・景設計事務所
e. 阿部順一郎
f. ㈱創研
g. 成田信勝
h. 中世に活躍した西洋の帆船をモデルに製作。海辺で自由な発想のもとに遊べる帆船型アスレチック。
i. 木材（レッドウッド，特殊防腐処理したダグラスモミ）／耐候性鋼材（コールテン鋼）
j. ㈱創研

a. SHONAN-KAIGAN SEASIDE PARK SAILBOAT SLIDE
b. Fujisawa-shi, Kanagawa
c. Kanagawa Pre.
d. Sanki-Kei Landscape Office
e. Junichiro Abe
f. SOUKEN Co., Ltd.
g. Nobukatsu Narita
h. Modeled after the western style ships the middle ages, this allows for athletic play and dreams along the seaside.
i. Redwood and climate-resisten hardeners
j. SOUKEN Co., Ltd.

a. 東京競馬場の木馬と遊具
b. 東京都府中市
c. 日本競馬施設㈱
d. ㈱ブレック研究所
e. 黛卓郎
f. 清水津設㈱＋㈱富士植木
g. 成田信勝
h. ダービースクエアの一部に設置された象徴的な木馬と自然に一周してしまうアスレチック的な遊具類。
i. 木材（特殊防腐処理されたダグラスモミ）
j. ㈱創研

a. WOOD HORSE AND PLAYTHINGS AT TOKYO RACETRACK
b. Fuchu-shi, Tokyo
c. Japan Horse Race Facitity Co., Ltd.
d. PREC Institute Co., Ltd.
e. Takuro Mayuzumi
f. SHIMIZU CORPORATION, FUJI UEKI Co., Ltd.
g. Nobukatsu Narita
h. The athletic playthings in Derby Square are properly symbolic, especially the wooden horse.
i. Climater-resistant wood
j. SOUKEN Co., Ltd.

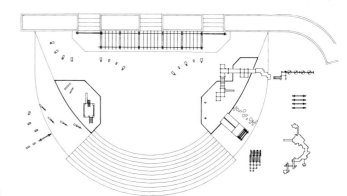

a. 東あずま公園・健康づくりコーナー
b. 東京都墨田区
c. 墨田区
d. 墨田区公園河川課
e. ㈱創研
f. 京成バラ園芸㈱
g. 島田昭治
h. 子供たちも大人も楽しめる健康遊具，上肢運動から始まり，体幹運動へ。そして下肢運動で終わる設計。
i. 木材（特殊防腐処理したダグラスモミ）
j. ㈱創研

a. HIGASHI AZUMA PARK HEALTH CORNER
b. Sumida-ku, Tokyo
c. Sumida Ward
d. Park Section, Sumida Ward
e. SOUKEN Co., Ltd.
f. Keisei-Rose-Gardening Co., Ltd.
g. Shoji Shimada
h. A place where children, and adults as well, can play. Exercise begins with the upper body and progresses through the middle body and legs.
i. Climate-resistant wood
j. SOUKEN Co., Ltd.

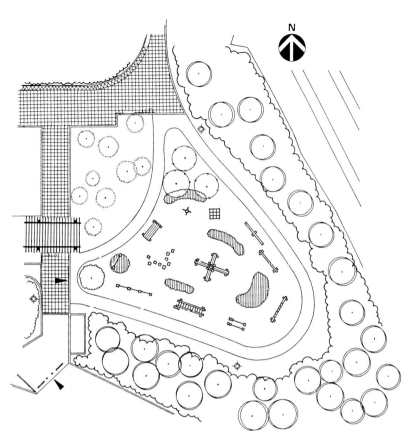

a. ガリバー滑り台
b. 滋賀県高島町
c. 高島町
d. 小笠原弘人
e. 小笠原弘人
f. 内田工業㈱
h. 設置場所が傾斜地であり，その自然環境を生かした巨大な滑り台や砦遊びを複合した遊具。
i. 米松，ステンレス
j. 内田工業㈱

a. GULLIVER'S SLIDE
b. Takashima-cho, Siga
c. Takashima
d. Hiroto Ogasawara
e. Hiroto Ogasawara
f. UCHIDA INDUSTRIAL Co., Ltd.
h. The design of this giant slide and fort was matched to the inclined slope of the land.
i. Douglas fir and stainless steel
j. UCHIDA INDUSTRIAL Co., Ltd.

a. 木製遊具
b. 愛知県岡崎市
c. 岡崎市
d. 宮武美弘
e. 小笠原弘人
f. 内田工業㈱
h. 築山に設けられた広場のシンボル的な遊具。シンボル性を高めるため，最上部に風見鶏を配置した
i. 木材／ステンレス／FRP材
j. 内田工業㈱

a. PLAYING LOT
b. Okazaki-shi, Aichi
c. Okazaki city
d. Yoshihiro Miyatake
e. Hiroto Ogasawara
f. UCHIDA INDUSTRIAL Co., Ltd.
h. At the top of this wooden ride is a chicken-shaped weathervane. This is constructed atop a man-made mountain
i. Wood, stainless, FRP
j. UCHIDA INDUSTRIAL Co., Ltd.

a. 塩釜公園の滑り台
b. 東京都港区
c. 港区
d. 港区土木部
e. 波多野隆
f. ㈱日比谷花壇造園土木
g. 島田昭治
h. 商業地域にあるこの児童公園は思わず誘い込まれ
　そうな温い雰囲気をもつ木製遊具の公園。
i. 木材（特殊防腐処理されたダグラスモミとレッドウッ
　ド）
j. ㈱創研

a. SHIOGAMA PARK'S SLIDE
b. Minato-ku, Tokyo
c. Minato Ward
d. Minato Ward, Park Section
e. Takashi Hatano
f. Hibiya Garden & Landscape Co., Ltd.
g. Shoji Shimada
h. The wood construction in this park, which is situ-
　ated in a business area, offers an exceptionally
　warm atmosphere.
i. Redwood and Douglas fir
j. SOUKEN Co., Ltd.

a. 公園遊具
b. 東京都港区
c. 港区
d. 港区ライオンズクラブ
e. 港区土木部
f. 京急緑地建設㈱
g. 島田昭治
h. 砂場，ブランコ，滑り台の三種の神器に加えられた
　スプリング遊具。遊びの世界が大きく広がる。
j. ㈱創研

a. PARK TOYS
b. Minato-ku, Tokyo
c. Minato Ward
d. Lions Club of Minato-ku
e. Minato Ward, Park Section
f. Keikyu Ryokuchi Construction
g. Shoji Shimada
h. Spring boards, which will grow styles of play,
　added to a sandbox, swing and slide
j. SOUKEN Co., Ltd.

a. 桜道公園・遊具
b. 神奈川県伊勢原市
c. 伊勢原市
d. 荻原信行，東畑建築事務所
e. 荻原信行，東畑建築事務所
f. 三井建設・岩崎工務店共同企業体
g. SS現像所
h. 遊具を環状に配置することにより更に大きな遊具に
　 発展したり，複合的な次の遊びが発生する。
i. コンクリート打放／木
j. ㈱東畑建築事務所東京事務所

a. SAKURAMICHI (Cherry blossom way) PLAY-
　 ING LOT
b. Isehara-shi, Kanagawa
c. Isehara City
d. Nobuyuki Hagiwara, Tohata Associates, Architects
e. Nobuyuki Hagiwara, Tohata & Associates, Archi-
　 tects
f. Mitsui Iwasaki J.V.
g. SS-Genzosyo
h. Putting out laeger playing lot toys will develop new
　 styles of play
i. Concrete and wood
j. Tohata Associates, Architects

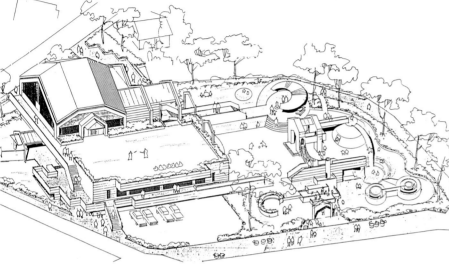

a. 遊具
b. 福岡県海の中道公園
c. 建設省
d. 山崎猛
e. 松原善郎
h. アーベンチャートリムの耐候性と耐水性に対する抜群の強さを、親水公園に生かした。
i. 木粉と熱可塑性樹脂を原料とした、複合強化プラスチック。
j. 凸版印刷㈱

a. PLAYING LOT
b. Fukuoka-shi, Fukuoka
c. The Ministry of Construction
d. Takeshi Yamazaki
e. Yoshio Matsubara
h. This adventurous construct is built to with stand the sea air and go well in the ocean environment.
i. Molded wood and laminates, reinforced plastic
j. TOPPAN PRINTING Co., Ltd.

a. ザイル クライミング
b. 埼玉県安行市出羽公園
c. 川口市川口
e. コンラッド・ローランド（西ドイツ）
f. ㈱コトブキ
g. 安藤孝
h. 多年層の子供達が同時に遊べ，まさかの時でも安
　全なようにロープの組み方が設計されている。
i. 鋼線被覆ロープ，丸パイプの支柱
j. ㈱コトブキ

a. CLIMBING
b. Kawaguchi-shi, Saitama
c. Kawaguchi City
e. Conrad Roland (West Germany)
f. KOTOBUKI Co., Ltd.
g. Takashi Ando
h. Children of different ages can play here. The ropes
　are designed to be safe in any situations.
i. Fiber rope and pipe
j. KOTOBUKI Co., Ltd.

a. アーチ遊具
b. 神奈川県横須賀市
c. 神奈川県
d. ㈱都市計画研究所
e. 樋口政善
g. 島田昭治
i. ヘムロックの集成材，パイプは粉体塗装仕上げ，ア
　ーチの表面はイエローシーダー材。
j. ㈱創研

a. THE ARCH
b. Yokosuka-shi, Kanagawa
c. Kanagawa Pre.
d. Toshikeikaku kenkyujo Co., Ltd.
e. Masayoshi Higuchi
g. Shoji Shimada
i. Hemlock, cedar, coated pipe
j. SOUKEN Co., Ltd.

a. ドラゴンシーソー
b. 愛知県名古屋市
c. 名古屋市
d. 小笠原弘人
e. 神谷直浩
f. 内田工業㈱
h. 中国的というテーマに基づき，人々を空想の世界に
　誘う目的でデザインした。
i. 鋼材／耐候性集成材／花崗岩／銅板
j. 内田工業㈱

a. THE DRAGON
b. Nagoya-shi, Aichi
c. Nagoya City
d. Hiroto Ogasawara
e. Naohiro Kamiya,
f. UCHIDA INDUSTRIAL Co., Ltd.
h. A Chinese style design meant to draw people into
　the world of make-believe.
i. Copper plate, granite, Climate-resistant materials.
j. UCHIDA INDUSTRIAL Co., Ltd.

a. ゴリラの親子
b. 埼玉県加須市
c. 住宅・都市整備公団
d. 栗原国男
e. 石松良介
f. 三井物産林業㈱
g. 栗原国男
h. モニュメンタルで，子供達から愛着を持たれる遊具
　として計画した。
i. 杉丸太３００ミリ～５００ミリ径
j. ㈱あい造園設計事務所

a. THE GORILLA
b. Kazo-shi, Saitama
c. Housing and Urban Development Corporation
d. Kunio Kurihara
e. Ryosuke Ishimatsu
f. Mitsui Bussan Ringyo Co., Ltd.
g. Kunio Kurihara
h. A monument that children grow to love.
i. Cedar, 300-500mm width
j. Ai Landscape Planning Co., Ltd.

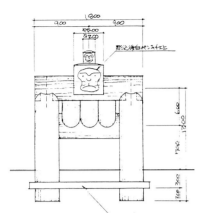

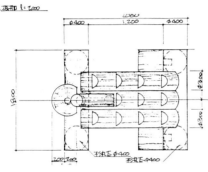

a. 池袋の時計塔
b. 東京都豊島区
c. 池袋西口開発委員会
d. 西沢健
e. 朝倉則幸，東亮，サウンドスケープ（時報担当）
f. ㈱ダイチ
g. 仲佐写真事務所
h. 時報に環境音楽を導入した都市風景の中の置時計
i. チタン，コールテン鋼，ステンレス，アルミニューム，黒御影石
j. ㈱GK設計

a. IKEBUKURO STATION WEST EXIT "TIME SQUARE"
b. Toshima-ku, Tokyo
c. Ikebukuro Nishi-Guchi Development Committee
d. Takeshi Nishizawa
e. Noriyuki Asakura, Ryo Higashi, Soundscape
f. DAICHI Co., Ltd.
g. T. Nacàsa & Partners
h. A clock that announces the time and plays music of environmental comfortable.
i. Titanium, steel, stainlass, aluminum, black granite
j. GK Sekkei Associates

a. ポップ・スウォッチ・タワー
b. 東京都渋谷区
c. スウォッチ ジャパン
d. ダイアン・セイヤ
e. 三村静香
f. ㈱アルス
h. 定刻になると大都市のポップサウンドをテーマに，両面にある時計が飛び出し３６０度回転する。
j. ㈱アルス HED 事業部

a. POP SWATCH TOWER
b. Shibuya-ku, Tokyo
c. SWATCH JAPAN K. K.
d. Dianne Sayegh
e. Shizuka Mimura
f. ARUSU Co., Ltd.
h. Pleasant music befitting a major metropolis plays on the hour. Upon striking the hour the front and back faces open and revolve 360 degrees
j. ARUSU Co., Ltd.

a. 戸井町の時計塔
b. 北海道戸井町
c. 戸井町
e. ㈱ダイチ
g. 仲佐写真事務所
j. ㈱ダイチ

a. CLOCK TOWER
b. Toi-machi, Hokkaido
c. Toi
e. DAICHI Co., Ltd.
g. T. Nacàsa & Partners
i. Stainless
j. DAICHI Co., Ltd.

a. 碧南の時計塔
b. 愛知県碧南市
e. 黒瀬渉行
g. 仲佐写真事務所
i. ステンレス
j. ㈱ダイチ

a. CLOCK TOWER
b. Hekinan-shi, Aichi
e. Tadayuki Kurose
g. T. Nacàsa & Partners
j. DAICHI Co., Ltd.

a. ゴルフ場の時計塔
b. 埼玉県比企郡
c. 高坂カントリークラブ
d. 鹿島建設㈱
e. ㈱イリア設計部
f. ㈱イリア設計部
g. 佐藤幸雄
h. シンボルとしての時計塔。平坦な芝生のゴルフ場の空間を引き締めている。緑とウッド材が周辺にマッチしている。
i. ソーラー時計／カルフォルニアレッドウッド材
j. ㈱創研

a. GOLF COURSE CLOCK TOWER
b. Hiki-gun, Saitama
c. Kosaka Country Club
d. KAJIMA Corporation
e. Design Department, Ilya Corporation
f. Ilya Corporation
g. Yukio Sato
h. A wooden clock tower goes well with the flat expanses of the course lawn
i. Solar-powered clock, California redwood
j. SOUKEN Co., Ltd.

a. やすらぎの里・カリオン
b. 茨城県那珂郡
c. 緒川町
d. 三貴・景観設計事務所
e. 金川敏美
f. 岡部工務店
g. 神山郁夫
i. レッドウッド／洋鐘・真ちゅう
j. ㈱創研

a. CARILLON CLOCK TOWER, PEACEFUL VILLAGE "YASURAGI-NO-SATO"
b. Naka-gun, Ibaraki
c. Ogawa
d. Sanki Kei Landscape Office
e. Toshimi Kanagawa
f. Okabe Koumuten Co., Ltd.
g. Ikuo Kamiyama
i. Redwood, bell (brass)
j. SOUKEN Co., Ltd.

a. 金杉台団地の時計塔
b. 千葉県船橋市
c. 住宅・都市整備公団
d. 戸田芳樹
e. 小峰貴芳
f. ㈱団地サービス
g. 伊藤直博
i. コンクリート／鍛鉄造形
j. ㈱戸田芳樹＋風景計画

a. CLOCK TOWER IN THE ESTATE SQUARE
b. Funabashi-shi, Chiba
c. Housing & Urban Debelopment Corporation
d. Yoshiki Toda
e. Toda Yoshiki & Fukei Keikaku Associates, Kiyoshi Shimakawa, Takayoshi Komine
f. Danchi Service Co., Ltd.
i. Naohiro Itoh
i. Tile, concrete
j. Toda Yoshiki & Fukei Keikaku Associates

a. 時計塔
b. 埼玉県大井町
c. 大井町特定土地区画整理事業組合
e. 影森文美
f. ㈱サカエ
g. 中山和男
i. ステンレス
j. ㈱サカエ

a. CLOCK TOWER
b. Ohi-machi, Saitama
c. Ohi
e. Ayami Kagemori
f. Sakae Co., Ltd.
g. Kazuo Nakayama
i. Stainless
j. Sakae Co., Ltd.

a. 時計塔
b. 神奈川県川崎市
c. 川崎市環境保全局
e. 荻野達雄
f. ㈱サカエ
g. 加藤廣史
i. ステンレス
j. ㈱サカエ

a. CLOCK TOWER
b. Kawasaki-shi, Kanagawa
c. Kawasaki City
e. Tatsuo Ogino
f. Sakae Co., Ltd.
g. Hiroshi Kato
i. Stainless steel
j. Sakae Co., Ltd.

a. 名古屋港の時計
b. 愛知県名古屋市
e. 黒瀬渉行
g. 仲佐写真事務所
h. 三面使用の時計本体の下部に名古屋港をイメージするカモメのオブジェを組み合わせた
i. ステンレスの鏡面仕上げ
j. ㈱ダイチ

a. CLOCK, NAGOYA PORT
b. Nagoya-shi, Aichi
e. Tadayuki Kurose
g. T. Nacàsa & Partners
h. This three-sided clock makes the sea gull, which is Nagoya Port's symbol, its theme
i. Polished stainless steel
j. DAICHI Co., Ltd.

a. 時計塔
b. 愛知県名古屋市
c. 中日新聞社会事業団
e. 小笠原弘人
f. 内田工業㈱
h. ソーラーシステムを応用したチャイムの音がひびきわたる
i. 花崗岩/コンクリート
j. 内田工業㈱

a. CLOCK TOWER
b. Nagoya-shi, Aichi
c. THE CHUNICHI SHINBUN Social Work Group
e. Hiroto Ogasawara
f. UCHIDA INDUSTRIAL Co., Ltd.
h. This clock chime reverberates with the solar system
i. Granite and concrete
j. UCHIDA INDUSTRIAL Co., Ltd.

a. 七沢自然公園の時計塔
b. 神奈川県厚木市
c. 厚木市
d. スペース・デザインハッピー，石井敏和
e. 石井敏和，和田誠治
f. ㈱ニュー・アイ
g. 和田誠治
j. スペース・デザインハッピー

a. CLOCK TOWER, NATURAL FACILITY NANAS-
   AWA
b. Atsugi-shi, Kanagawa
c. Atsugi City
d. Space Design Happy Co., Ltd., Toshikazu Ishii
e. Toshikazu Ishii, Seiji Wada
f. New Idea Co., Ltd.
g. Seiji Wada
j. Space Design Happy Co., Ltd.

a. 小牛田駅開発の時計塔
b. 宮城県小牛田町
d. ㈱河北エンジニアリング
e. 黒瀬歩行
g. 仲佐写真事務所
i. ステンレス鏡面仕上げ
j. ㈱ダイチ

a. CLOCK TOWER, OGOTA STATION
b. Ogota-machi, Miyagi
c. Ogota
e. Kahoku Engineering Co., Ltd.
f. Tadayuki Kurose
g. T. Nacàsa & Partners
i. Stainless
j. DAICHI Co., Ltd.

a. 日時計
b. 愛知県名古屋市
c. 名古屋市
d. 小笠原弘人
e. 松本美智子
f. 内田工業㈱
h. 恒久的な素材を用いスケール感のある表現をした。
　 時刻表示部はスツールとして利用できる。
i. 花崗岩／ステンレス
j. 内田工業㈱

a. Sundial
b. Nagoya-shi, Aichi
c. Nagoya City
d. Hiroto Ogasawara
e. Michiko Matsumoto
f. UCHIDA INDUSTRIAL Co., Ltd.
h. Durable materials lend a feeling of grand scale to the sundial, which tells of the gradual flow of time
i. Granite, stainless
j. UCHIDA INDUSTRIAL Co., Ltd.

a. 日時計
b. 愛知県名古屋市
c. 中日新聞社会事業団
d. 小笠原弘人
e. 黒野誠一
f. 内田工業㈱
h. ステンレス部のうつり込みにより空間が分割されず、モニュメントとしての要素も含まれている。
i. 花崗岩／ステンレス
j. 内田工業㈱

a. SUNDIAL
b. Nagoya-shi, Aichi
c. THE CHUNICHI SHINBUN Social Work Group
d. Hiroto Ogasawara
e. Seiichi Kurono
f. UCHIDA INDUSTRIAL Co., Ltd.
h. The stainless steel preserves the feeling of openness and creates the ambience of a monument
i. Granite, stainless steel
j. UCHIDA INDUSTRIAL Co., Ltd.

a. 杉戸駅前広場の日時計
b. 埼玉県杉戸町
c. 埼玉県杉戸土地区画整理事務所
d. 日本技術開発㈱、田村利久
e. 住谷正巳
f. ㈱ウォーター デザイン
i. ステンレス、御影石
j. ㈱ウォーター デザイン

a. SUNDIAL, IN SUGITO STATION SQUARE
b. Sugito-machi, Saitama
c. Sugito
d. JAPAN ENGINEERING CONSULTANTS Co., Ltd.
e. Masami Sumitani
i. Granite, stainless steel
j. WATER DESIGN Co., Ltd.

a. 太陽のある広場・日時計
b. 東京都足立区入谷中央公園
c. 足立区
d. ㈱カーター・アート環境計画
e. 富田真平
f. ㈱ウォーターデザイン
h. 午前の陽を受ける面と午後の陽を受ける面を石の中で交差させることで時を内臓する形にした。
i. 御影石／ステンレス
j. ㈱ウォーターデザイン

a. SUN SQUARE & SUNDIAL
b. Adachi-ku, Tokyo
c. Adachi Ward
d. KARTER ART LANDSCAPE CONSULTANTS, Co., Ltd.
e. Shinpei Tomita
f. WATER DESIGN Co., Ltd.
h. The rocks are arranged to collect morning and afternoon sunlight and express the time
i. Granite, stainless steel
j. WATER DESIGN Co., Ltd.

a. 城山緑地の日時計
b. 福岡県北九州市
c. 公害防止事業団
d. 清水一雄
e. 住谷正巳, ㈱ウォーター　デザイン
f. ㈱ウォーター　デザイン
i. ステンレス/御影石
j. ㈱ウォーターデザイン

a. SUNDIAL, SHIROYAMA RYOKUCHI PARK
b. Kita-kyushu-shi, Fukuoka
c. The Environmental Pollution Service Corporation
d. Kazuo Shimizu
f. WATER DESIGN Co., Ltd.
i. Stainless, granite
j. WATER DESIGN Co., Ltd.

a. 松原公園・日時計
b. 大分県別府市
c. 別府市
e. ㈱ウォーターデザイン, 住谷正己
f. ㈱ウォーターデザイン
i. 御影石／ステンレス
j. ㈱ウォーターデザイン

a. SUNDIAL
b. Beppu-shi, Ohita
c. Beppu City
e. WATER DESIGN Co., Ltd., Masami Sumitani
f. WATER DESIGN Co., Ltd.
i. Granite, stainless steel
j. WATER DESIGN Co., Ltd.

a. 日時計
b. 福井県福井市
c. 福井県
d. ㈱宮本設計事務所
e. 富田真平
f. ㈱ウォーターデザイン
i. 御影石／ステンレス
j. ㈱ウォーターデザイン

a. SUNDIAL IN IKUHISA PARK
b. Fukui-shi, Fukui
c. Fukui Pre.
d. Miyamoto Engineer Architects Ltd.
e. Shinpei Tomita
f. WATER DESIGN Co., Ltd.
i. Granite, stainless
j. WATER OESIGN Co., Ltd.

a. 十二支の彫刻
b. 山梨県甲府市
c. エル・西銀座商店街
d. 田渕照久
e. 浦野八重子
f. ㈱コトブキ
g. 安藤孝
h. 中堅彫刻作家による十二支のブロンズ像。商店街のアイドルとして子供達から大人にまで親しまれ愛され、街の活性化に役立っている。
i. ブロンズ
j. ㈱コトブキ

a. TWELVE-LIMBED MONUMENTS
b. Kofu-shi, Yamanashi
c. L Nishi-ginza Ave.
d. Teruhisa Tabuchi
e. Yaeko Urano
f. KOTOBUKI Co., Ltd.
g. Takashi Ando
h. The twelve-part sculpture in bronze by a sculptor of middle standing. Loved by children and adults alike, this work is helping to energize city activity.
i. Bronze
j. KOTOBUKI Co., Ltd.

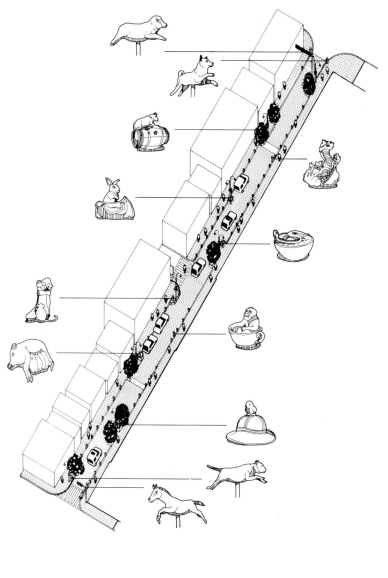

a.「だいち」0からのかたち
b. 広島市
c. 広島市
d. 岡本敦生，西雅秋
e. 岡本敦生，西雅秋
f. 岡本敦生，西雅秋
g. 岡本敦生
h. 彫刻が単体で孤立するのではなく，彫刻空間の中に人々を引き込むことで生活空間全体を作品化する。
i. 白御影石（真壁産）／コールテン・鋼板
j. 岡本敦生

a. STARTING FROM ZERO-"THE PLATEAU"
b. Hiroshima-shi, Hiroshima
c. Hiroshima City
d. Atsuo Okamoto, Masaaki Nishi
e. Atsuo Okamoto, Masaaki Nishi
f. Atsuo Okamoto, Masaaki Nishi
g. Atsuo Okamoto
h. The sculpture is not an independent form in a space, but something which draws people in and makes the living space "artlike."
i. White granite, stainless steel
j. Atsuo Okamoto

a. 彫刻「道しるべ」
b. 岡山県倉敷市
c. 大原美術館
e. 速水史朗
f. 和泉屋石材
g. 石井直矢
h. 新館へのアプローチとして石彫をインスタレーションすることにより現代風の石庭が出現した。
i. 黒花崗岩
j. 速水史朗

a. "AQUAINTANCE ROAD"
b. Kurashiki-shi, Okayama
c. OHARA MUSEUM OF ART
e. Shiro Hayami
f. IZUMIYA Co., Ltd.
g. Naoya Ishi
h. A new style of rock garden was created by placing these sculptures along the approach to this building.
i. White granite
j. Shiro Hayami

a. 彫刻「生」
b. 千葉県浦安市
c. 順天堂大学
d. 有山登
e. 渡辺隆根，高野重文
f. 渡辺隆根，㈱清水建設
g. 渡辺隆根
h. 病院，建築の構築的な固さなどを考慮しやさしい感じと土からのびる生命感を出すことにつとめた。
i. 花崗岩（稲田石）
j. 渡辺隆根

a. SCULPTURE
b. Urayasu-shi, Chiba
c. Juntendo University
d. Noboru Ariyama
e. Takane Watanabe, Shigefumi Takano
f. Takane Watanabe, SHIMIZU CORPORATION
g. Takane Watanabe
h. The hospital and "hardness" of the construction were considered, and a feeling of ease and growth from the ground up was acheived.
i. Garnite
j. Takane Watanabe

a. 鷺舞の譜
b. 山口県山口市
c. 山口県
e. 澄川喜一
f. ㈱タカタ
i. 花崗岩（稲田石，高さ11m，ビシャン仕上げ）
j. ㈱タカタ

a. MONUMENT, THE DANCING HERON
b. Yamaguchi-shi, Yamaguchi
c. Yamaguchi City
e. Kiichi Sumikawa
f. Takata Co., Ltd.
g. Granite (Inada-ishi)
i. Granite
j. Takata Co., Ltd.

165

a. モニュメント
b. 大阪府大阪市
e. 岡山信也，アレッサンドロ・メンディニ
g. 仲佐写真事務所
h. 大阪駅のシンボルとして制作された
i. ステンレスの鏡面仕上げ
j. ㈱ダイチ

a. MONUMENT
b. Osaka-shi, Osaka
e. Shinya Okayama, Alessandro Mendini
g. T.Nacàsa & Partners
h. Created as Osaka's station
i. Stainless
j. DAICHI Co., Ltd.

a. モニュメント
b. 大阪府大阪市
e. 岡山伸也，アレッサ・メンディーニ
g. 仲佐写真事務所
h. 大阪駅前広場のシンボルとして制作された
i. ステンレス
j. ㈱ダイチ

a. MONUMENT
b. Osaka-shi, Osaka
e. Shinya Okayama, Alessandro Mendini
g. T.Nacàsa & Partners
h. Created as Osaka's station
i. Stainless
j. DAICHI Co., Ltd.

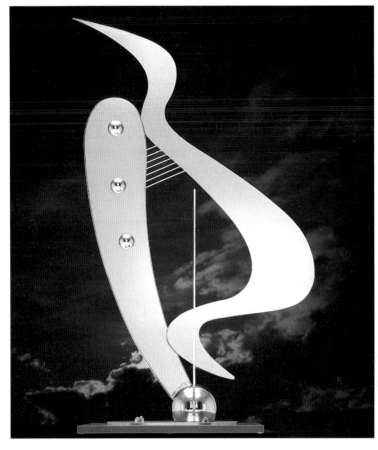

a. モニュメント
b. 茨城県古河市
c. 横山町商店街
d. 柳沼正典
e. 小林三千夫
f. ㈱コトブキ
g. 安藤孝
h. 地元産出の石材（ブルーファンタジーストーン）を使
　用。夜間には照明が入るようにした道しるべ。
i. 石／FRP
j. ㈱コトブキ

a. MONUMENT
b. Koga-shi, Ibaraki
c. Yokoyama-cho, Ave.
d. Masanori Yaginuma
e. Michio Kobayashi
f. KOTOBUKI Co., Ltd.
g. Takashi Ando
h. Native rock was used, and the design allows
　evening illumination to up the monument.
i. Stone, FRP
j. KOTOBUKI Co., Ltd.

a. 小瀬スポーツ公園モニュメント「かたらい」
b. 山梨県甲府市
c. 山梨県土木部都市計画課
d. 山梨県土木部　佐野修平＋日本技術開発　渡辺秀雄,
e. 日本技術開発㈱＋住谷正己
f. ㈱ウォーターデザイン
g. 住谷正己
h. 鳥をモチーフにした三体のモニュメントは様々な人々の温かい交流を象徴している。
i. ステンレス
j. ㈱ウォーターデザイン

a. KOSE SPORTS PARK MONUMENT
b. Kofu-shi, Yamanashi
c. Yamanashi Pre.
d. Shuhei Sano, Hideo Watanabe, Yamanashi Pre. Japan Engineering Consultants Co., Ltd.
e. Japan Engineering Consultants Co., Ltd.
f. WATER DESIGN Co., Ltd.
g. Masami Sumiya
h. Using birds as a symbol, this bodied monument represents the interaction of people
i. Stainless steel
j. WATER DESIGN Co., Ltd.

a. 檀一雄文学碑
b. 福岡県柳川市
c. 檀一雄文学碑建立委員会
d. 文学碑建立委員会
e. 横沢英一
f. 梅崎石材産業，横沢英一
g. 梅崎文夫
h. 柳川水路，周辺の緑，風のイメージにより檀一雄の人となりとロマンをデザインした。
i. 花崗岩（徳山黒御影石）
j. 横沢英一

a. MONUMENT TO KAZUO DAN
b. Yanagawa-shi, Fukuoka
c. Monument Foundation Committee
e. Hidekazu Yokozawa
f. Umezaki Sekizai, Hidekazu Yokozawa
g. Fumio Umezaki
h. Designed to reflect the Yanagawa waterway, surrounding greenery, and the spirit of Kazuo Dan's work.
i. Tokuyama black granite
j. Hidekazu Yokozawa

a. 田川高校・新築記念碑
b. 長野県塩尻市
c. 長野県
d. 長野県施設課
e. 横沢英一＋ランドスケープデザインコンサルタント
f. 横沢英一、黒髪石材㈱
g. 小原順
h. 新設高校のキャンパス計画の一環として設計し、単体の彫刻でなく施設としての面的存在を考えた。
i. 花崗岩（徳山御影石）／おかめささ／砂利
j. ㈱ランドスケープ デザイン コンサルタント

a. MONUMENT TO THE NEW TAGAWA HIGH SCHOOL
b. Shiojiri-shi, Nagano
c. Nagano Pre.
d. Nagano Pre.
e. Hidekazu Yokozawa
f. Hidekazu Yokozawa, Kurokami-sekizai Inc.
g. Jun Ohara
h. The campus was planned as one total environment, and this sculpture was meant as a facility in itself.
i. Granite, sand
j. LANDSCAPE DESIGN CONSULTANTS Co., Ltd.

a. 彫刻「北風」
b. 新潟県新潟市
e. 高橋清
f. 高橋清
g. 脇坂進
h. 雪国の烈しい自然の変貌の中で生まれる幻想と研ぎ澄まされた感性を白御影石で造形化した。
i. 白御影石
j. 高橋清

a. SCULPTURE
b. Niigata-shi, Niigata
e. Kiyoshi Takahashi
f. Kiyoshi Takahashi
g. Susumu Wakisaka
h. A place where nature and form coexist in everyday life ; an attempt to address the question of eternity and human existence.
i. White granite
j. Kiyoshi Takahashi

a. 神湊港モニュメント「わたる」
b. 東京都八丈島
c. 東京都
e. 富田真平＋㈱ウォーターデザイン
f. ㈱ウォーターデザイン
h. 厳しい自然環境での存在感と島外との交流を象徴
　　する作品。
i. 白御影石
j. ㈱ウォーターデザイン

a. MONUMENT, SHIN-MINATO
b. Hachizyo-jima, Tokyo
c. Tokyo Metropolis
e. Sinpei Tomita, WATER DESIGN Co., Ltd.
f. WATER DESIGN Co., Ltd.
h. Symbolic of the harsh environment and relation to
　　areas beyond the island.
i. White granite
j. WATER DESIGN Co., Ltd.

a. 彫刻「希望と瞑想の場」
b. 東京都世田谷区総合グランド
c. 世田谷区
e. 高橋清
f. 高橋清
g. 毛利秀之，脇坂進
h. 都市生活の日常性の中で自然と造形が調和する
　　「場」を作り，人間の存在と永遠性を問いなおした
　　かった。
i. 白御影石
j. 高橋清

a. SCULPTURE
b. Setagaya-ku, Tokyo
c. Setagaya Ward
e. Kiyoshi Takahashi
f. Kiyoshi Takahashi
g. Hideyuki Mori, Susumu Wakisaka
h. A monument which questions human existence and
　　eternity and Province a place where nature and
　　created form blend into everyday city life
i. White granite
j. Kiyoshi Takahashi

a. 彫刻「ぬし」
b. 兵庫県尼崎市中央公園
c. 尼崎市
e. 速水史朗
f. 泉和屋石材，＝水社
g. 安斎重男
h. 尼崎市の街並のイメージを更によくするために水の
　神で美しい水のある街を表現した。
i. 花崗岩
j. 速水史朗

a. SCULPTURE
b. Amagasaki-shi, Hyogo
c. Amagasaki City
e. Shiro Hayami
f. IZUMIYA, SANSUI-SHA Co., Ltd.
g. Sigeo Anzai
h. Amagasaki city mall improved its image with this
　sculpture of the sea god, expressing the motif of
　beautiful water.
i. Granite
j. Shiro Hayami

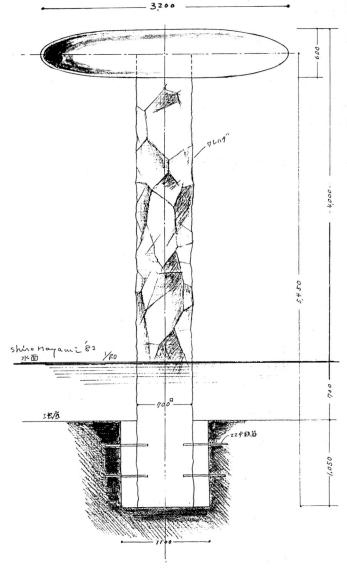

a. 春日部駅前・記念碑
b. 埼玉県春日部市
c. 春日部市
d. 春日部市
e. 横沢英一+ランドスケープ デザイン コンサルタント
f. 横沢英一，黒髪石材㈱
g. 横沢英一
h. 駅周辺の将来像との調和，太陽と人の動きの変化の美しさ，地耐力ゼロの地盤の基礎構造を考えた。
i. 花崗岩（徳山御影石）
j. ㈱ランドスケープ デザイン コンサルタント

a. KASUKABE STATIONFRONT MEMORIAL MONUMENT
b. Kasukabe-shi, Saitama
c. Kasukabe City
d. Kasukabe City
e. Hidekazu Yokozawa, LANDSCAPE DESIGN CONSULTANTS Co.,Ltd.
f. Hidekazu Yokozawa, Kurokami-sekizai Co., Ltd.
g. Hidekazu Yokozawa
h. Built to go with the future changes in the surrounding area, this symbolizes the beauty of sun and people and as they move and change.
i. Granite
j. LANDSCAPE DESIGN CONSULTANTS Co.,Ltd.

a. 「翔ぶ」
b. 静岡県御殿場市
c. 積機技研工業㈱
d. ㈱東京グラフィックデザイナーズ　畑雅大
e. 佐久間義敬
f. ㈱アルス
h. 赤い風見は風に向って回り，90個の青黄のカップが風に乗って螺旋を描き雄大な動きを表す。
i. ステンレススチール
j. ㈱アルスHED事業部

a. "FLIGHT"
b. Gotenba-shi, Shizuoka
c. SEIKI GIKEN KOGYO Co., Ltd.
d. Masao Hata, TOKYO GRAPHIC DESIGNERS INC.
e. Ghikei Sakuma
f. ARUSU Co., Ltd.
h. The red weather vane turns to face the wind and ninety individual yellow and blue cups move in a great spiral expression.
i. Stainless steel
j. ARUSU Co., Ltd.

a. モニュメント「こころ」
b. 埼玉県深谷市
c. 深谷市区画整理課
e. 室田秀男
f. ㈱サカエ
g. ㈱サカエ　中山和男
i. ブロンズ／擬石／黒御影石
j. ㈱サカエ

a. MONUMENT
b. Fukaya-shi, Saitama
c. Fukaya City
e. Hideo Murota
f. SAKAE Co., Ltd.
g. Kazuo Nakayama, SAKAE Co.,Ltd.
i. Bronze, black granite, imitation stone
j. SAKAE Co., Ltd.

a. 彫刻「祖・魂・蔵」
b. 東京都府中市博物館
c. 府中市
d. 石本建築設計事務所
e. 速水史朗
f. 和泉屋石材
g. 速水史朗
h. 府中市市博物館の守護神として三点の彫刻を配した。
i. 黒花崗岩
j. 速水史朗

a. SCULPTURE
b. Fuchu-shi, Tokyo
c. Fuchu City
d. Ishimoto Associates Co., Ltd.
e. Shiro Hayami
f. IZUMIYA
g. Shiro Hayami
h. Fuchu city erected these three sculptings around the musuem.
i. Black granite
j. Shiro Hayami

a. SCULPTURE
b. Fuchu-shi, Tokyo
c. Fuchu City
d. Ishimoto Associates Co., Ltd.
e. Shiro Hayami
f. IZUMIYA
府中市市博物館の守護神として三点の彫刻を配し

a. 彫刻「太陽の門」
b. 兵庫県神戸市
c. 神戸市
e. 速水史朗
g. 畠山乗
h. 街角に立つ石彫は神戸市民との触れ合いに役立っている。太陽がこの門に差し込む瞬間が美しい。
i. 花崗岩
j. 速水史朗

a. "SUNGATE"
b. Kobe-shi, Hyogo
c. Kobe City
e. Shiro Hayami
g. Takashi Hatakeyama
h. These external facing stone carvings assist in the interaction of Kobe's populace. The monument when the sun pierces the gates is particulary beautiful.
i. Granite
j. Shiro Hayami

a. 風の広場・モニュメント
b. 東京都足立区
c. 足立区
d. (株)カーター・アート環境計画
e. 住谷正己
f. (株)ウォーターデザイン
i. ステンレス
j. (株)ウォーターデザイン

a. WIND SQUARE MONUMENT
b. Adachi-ku, Tokyo
c. Adachi Ward
d. KARTER ART LANDSCAPE CONSULTANTS Co., Ltd.
e. Masami Sumitani
f. WAETR DESIGN Co.,Ltd.
i. Stainless
j. WAETR DESIGN Co.,Ltd.

a. 風の導標
b. 富山県婦中町
c. IDEC 和泉電機富山製作所
d. 佐久間義敬
e. 佐久間義敬
f. 川崎重工業(株)
g. 佐久間義敬
h. IDEC の「I」をシンボル化し, 風を受けて回転すると翼が水平になり, 再び元の形に戻る。
i. ステンレススチール
j. サクマ デザイン スタジオ

a. WIND VANE
b. Fuchu-machi,Toyama
c. IDEC IZUMI TOYAMA Co., Ltd.
d. Ghikei Sakuma
e. Ghikei Sakuma
f. KAWASAKI HEAVY INDUSTRIES Ltd.
g. Ghikei Sakuma
h. The "I" of IDEC is symbolized in this wind vane. When it turns the wings flatten, then returns to an upright position.
i. Stainless steel
j. Sakuma Design Studio Inc.

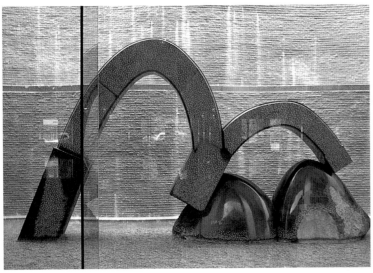

a. グランドヒル市ケ谷「虹の島影」
b. 東京都新宿区市ケ谷
c. 防衛庁
d. 関根伸夫＋環境美術研究所
e. ㈱樟建築設計
f. ㈱タカタ
g. 広田治雄
h. シティホテルのロビーを豊かな空間として演出した庭園。虹や島影を模し日本庭園の形式を取り入れた。
i. 大蔵石（宮城県産）／黒御影石（アフリカ産）
j. 環境美術研究所

a. SCULPTURE "RAINBOW SHADOW OF ISLAND"
b. Shinzyuku-ku, Tokyo
c. The Defence Agency
d. Nobuo Sekine & Environment Art Studio
e. Azusa Associates
f. Takata Co., Ltd.
g. Haruo Hirota
h. The garden makes the lobby of this hotel a rich expression of space. The rainbow and island scene are incorporated into a Japanese garden setting.
i. African black granite, Miyagi
j. Environment Art Studio

a. 砧公園の「風景の門」
b. 東京都世田谷区砧公園
c. 世田谷区
d. 関根伸夫＋環境美術研究所
e. 関根伸夫
f. ㈱タカタ，千歳金属㈱
g. 広田治雄
h. 砧ファミリー・パークの入口を飾るモニュメント門とし
　てデザインした
i. 白御影石（稲田石）/ステンレス
j. 環境美術研究所

a. MONUMENT
b. Setagaya-ku, Tokyo
c. Setagaya Ward
d. Nobuo Sekine & Environment Art Studio Inc.
e. Nobuo Sekine
f. TAKATA Co., Ltd., Chitose Kinzoku Co., Ltd.
g. Haruo Hirota
h. A monument design for the entrance to Kinuta
　family park
i. White granite and stainlass
j. Environment Art Studio Inc.

a. 筑波北部工業団地モニュメント
b. 茨城県 つくば市
c. 財団法人茨城県開発公社
d. 高瀬昭男
e. 高瀬昭男
f. 空間造形研究所
g. 紀善久
i. ステンレス
j. ㈱空間造形研究所

a. Mounyment in Tsukuba Northern Business
　and Research Park
b. Tsukuba-shi, Ibaraki
c. Ibaraki Pretectural Development Corporation.
d. Akio Takase
e. Akio Takase
f. Urban Space Art Studio Inc.
g. Yoshihisa Kino
i. Stainless
j. Urban Space Art Studio Inc.

a. 彫刻「門」
b. 兵庫県神戸市
c. 神戸市
e. 速水史朗
f. 和泉屋石材
g. 安斎重男
h. 石の彫刻の中を人が通り抜けられるようにして公園
　の中での人と石のふれあいを考えた
i. 花崗岩
j. 速水史朗

a. THE "GATE" SCULPTURE
b. Kobe-shi, Hyogo
c. Kobe City
e. Shiro Hayami
f. IZUMIYA
g. Shigeo Anzai
h. A place in the park where people can pass through
　and come in contact with the stone
i. Granite
j. Shiro Hayami

a. しおかぜ緑道の広場と彫刻
b. 千葉県浦安市
c. 浦安市
d. 村井寿夫
e. 八木ヨシオ，亀貝紘一郎，村井寿夫，原貴仁
f. ㈱東松園
g. 肥田葉子
h. 環境としての水と彫刻を調和させながら，この緑道
　のテーマを表現した広場
i. 御影石
j. あい造園設計事務所

a. SCULPTURE & SQUARE, SHIOKAZE (SEA
　BREEZE) GREEN PATH
b. Urayasu-shi, Chiba
c. Urayasu City
d. Hisao Murai
e. Yoshio Yagi, Koichiro Kamegai, Hisao Murai, Taka-
　hito Hara
f. Toshoen Co., Ltd.
g. Yoko Hida
h. The theme of water and sculpture harmoniously
　represent is the theme of this square on the
　pathway
i. Granite
j. Ai Landscape Planning Co., Ltd.

a. しおかぜ緑道の彫刻
b. 千葉県浦安市
c. 浦安市
d. 村井寿夫
e. 八木ヨシオ，村井寿夫
f. ㈱ノザワ
g. 肥田葉子
h. しおかぜ緑道のシンボルゾーンの入口に設置したメインテーマを象徴する彫刻
i. 黒御影石
j. あい造園設計事務所

a. SCULPTURE, SHIOKAZE (SEA BREEZE) GREEN PATH
b. Urayasu-shi, Chiba
c. Urayasu City
d. Hisao Murai
e. Yoshio Yagi, Hisao Murai
f. Nozawa Co., Ltd.
g. Yoko Hida
h. The sculpture at the entrance to Shiokaze pathway symbolizes the main theme of the area
i. Black granite
j. Ai Landscape Planning Co., Ltd.

a. 塩原西公園のモニュメント「天と地の会話」
b. 福岡県福岡市
c. 福岡市
e. 富田真平，㈱ウォーターデザイン
f. ㈱ウォーターデザイン
h. 区画整理事業の完成記念碑。天と大地からのささやきが融合し，誕生と発展の声がこだまする
i. 御影石
j. ㈱ウォーターデザイン

a. MONUMENT "HEAVEN & EARTH'S DIA-LOGUE"
b. Fukuoka-shi, Fukuoka
c. Fukuoka City
e. Shinpei Tomita, WATER DESIGN Co., Ltd.
f. WATER DESIGN Co., Ltd.
h. Here the words of heaven and earth are symbolically molded together.Commemoration of the division of the districts
i. Black granite
j. WATER DESIGN Co., Ltd.

a. 徳山国際カントリークラブのモニュメント
b. 山口県徳山市
c. 徳山国際カントリー倶楽部
d. 田辺武
e. 田辺武
f. 田辺武
g. 栗林和彦
i. 斑麗岩
j. 田辺武

a. MONUMENT
b. Tokuyama-shi, Yamaguchi
c. Tokuyama Kokusai Country Club
d. Takeshi Tanabe
e. Takeshi Tanabe
g. Kazuhiko Kuribayashi
i. Granite
j. Takeshi Tanabe

a. 希望ケ丘団地の彫刻
b. 東京都世田谷区
c. 住宅・都市整備公団
d. 戸田芳樹
e. 八木ヨシオ
f. ㈱団地サービス
g. 伊藤直博
j. ㈱戸田芳樹+風景計画

a. SCULPTURE, KIBOGAOKA SUN HILLS
b. Setagaya-ku, Tokyo
c. Housing & Urban Development Corporation
d. Yoshiki Toda
e. Toda Yoshiki & Fukei Keikaku Associates, Masayuki Nagi, Naohiro Itoh
f. Danchi Service Co., Ltd.
g. Naohiro Itoh
j. Toda Yoshiki & Fukei Keikaku Associates

a. 山口大学経済学部の記念碑
b. 山口県山口市
c. 鳳陽会
d. 田辺武
e. 田辺武
f. 田辺武
g. 栗林和彦
i. 自然石/芝生
j. 田辺武

a. COMMEMORATION MONUMENT
b. Yamaguchi-shi, Yamaguchi
c. Association of H Y
d. Takeshi Tanabe
e. Takeshi Tanabe
f. Takeshi Tanabe
g. Kazuhiko Kuribayashi
i. Natural stone, grass
j. Takeshi Tanabe

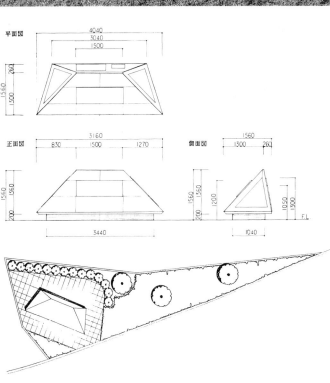

平面図

正面図　　側面図

a. 記念碑
b. 大分県大分市
c. 大分県区画整理協会
d. 脇百太郎
e. 松本克哉, 馬水幸広
g. 阿部恵治
i. ステンレス板/黒御影石平板/コンクリート
j. ㈱脇造園綜合設計

a. COMMEMORATION MONUMENT
b. Ohita-shi, Ohita
c. Street Improvement Association, Ohita Pre.
d. Hyakutaro Waki
e. Katsuya Matsumoto, Yukihiro Mamizu
g. Keiji Abe
i. Stainless, black granite and concrete
j. WAKI LAN DSCAPE DESIGN Co., Ltd.

a. 鼻岡邸のサイン
b. 広島県広島市
c. 鼻岡房夫
d. 佐々木著
e. 佐々木著
f. 飛島建設㈱
g. ㈱西日本写房
h. 流動的かつリズム感のあるアプローチとした
i. タイル/ステンシル切り抜き文字/スイッチ・インターホン/屋外灯/角パイプ
j. 佐々木著建築設計室

a. THE HANAOKA MANSION SIGN
b. Hiroshima-shi, Hirosima
c. Fusao Hanaoka
d. Itaru Sasaki
e. Itaru Sasaki
f. TOBISHIMA CORPORATION
g. Nishinihon Shabo Co., Ltd.
h. An approach sign that is both stylish and rhythmic.
i. Tile and stainless steel with engraved letters, interphone switch, square pipe illumination
j. Itaru Sasaki Architects Inc.

a. アークヒルズビルのサイン
b. 東京都港区
e. 黎インダストリアル　デザイン
g. 仲佐写真事務所
j. ㈱ダイチ

a. ARK HILLS BUILDING SIGN
b. Minato-ku, Tokyo
d. REI INDUSTRIAL DESIGN Co., Ltd.
e. DAICHI Co., Ltd.
g. T. Nacása & Partners
j. DAICHI Co., Ltd.

a. 北千住駅前・サイン
b. 東京都足立区北千住
c. 足立区
d. ㈱GK設計
e. 森田昌嗣, 中井川正道
f. ㈱スズオカ
g. 野口秀夫
h. 道案内とシンボルの役目に加え屏風をモチーフにした形は煩雑な広場にゆとりと秩序感を与える。
i. 耐候性鋼／桜御影石／板ガラス／ステンレス
j. ㈱スズオカ

a. MONUMENT & SIGN
b. Adachi-ku, Tokyo
c. Adachi Ward
d. GK Sekkei Associates
e. Yoshitsugu Morita, Masamichi Nakaigawa
f. Suzuoka Co., Ltd.
g. Hideo Noguchi
h. As a street sign and symbol, this sign allays the congestion of the area with its folding screen shape, suggesting both relaxation and order
i. Weather-resistant steel, cherry-stone granite, glass, stainless steel
j. Suzuoka Co., Ltd.

a. 大分コンパルホールのサイン
b. 大分県大分市
d. 内藤建築設計事務所
e. ㈱ダイチ
g. 仲佐写真事務所
j. ㈱ダイチ

a. SIGN
b. Ohita-shi, Ohita
d. Naito Associates Architects Engineers
e. DAICHI Co., Ltd.
g. T. Nacàsa & Partners
j. DAICHI Co., Ltd.

a. 長崎バイオパーク・サイン計画
b. 長崎県西彼杵郡
c. 長崎バイオパーク㈱
d. 朝永徹一
e. 千葉洋子, 沢田宏子
f. ㈱ティー・グラバー
g. ㈱ティー・グラバー
h. 21世紀の自然動植物公園として人と自然界の調和・共存を願いCIS・サイン計画に取り組んだ。
i. アルミ
j. ㈱ティー・グラバー

a. NAGASAKI BIO PARK SIGN PLANNING
b. Nishisonoki-gun, Nagasaki
c. NAGASAKI BIO PARK Co., Ltd.
d. Tetsuichi Tomonaga
e. Hiroko Chiba, Hiroko Sawada
f. T. GLOVER Co., Ltd.
g. T. GLOVER Co., Ltd.
h. A CIS sign design wishing for peaceful coexistence of people and the natural world. For a twenty-first century animal and plant park
i. Aluminum
j. T. GLOVER Co., Ltd.

a. 大崎駅東口再開発のサイン
b. 東京都品川区
d. 協立建築設計事務所
e. 協立建築設計事務所
g. 仲佐写真事務所
j. ㈱ダイチ

a. OSAKI STATION SIGN PLANNING
b. Shinagawa-ku, Tokyo
d. KYORITSU ASSOCIATES ARCHITECTS ENGINEERS
e. KYORITSU ASSOCIATES ARCHITECTS ENGINEERS
g. T. Nacása & Partners
j. DAICHI Co., Ltd.

a. グリーンピア津南のサイン
b. 新潟県中魚沼郡
c. 財年金福祉事業団, 財年金保養協会
d. ㈱日建設計
g. 仲佐写真事務所
j. ㈱ダイチ

a. GREEN PIER TSUNAN SIGN PLANNING
b. Tsunan-machi, Niigata
c. Annuity Welfare Enterprise, Annuity Recreation Association Foundation
d. NIKKEN SEKKEI Ltd.
g. T. Nacása & Partners
j. DAICHI Co., Ltd.

a. 安城駅前のサイン
b. 愛知県安城市
e. 環境開発研究所
g. 仲佐写真事務所
j. ㈱ダイチ

a. SIGN, ANZYO STATION
b. Anzyo-shi, Aichi
d. ENVIRONMENT DEVELOPMENT RESEARCH INC.
e. ENVIRONMENT DEVELOPMENT RESEARCH INC.
g. T. Nacása & Partner
j. DAICHI Co., Ltd.

a. 久喜総合文化会館のサイン
b. 埼玉県久喜市
c. 久喜市
d. 朝永徹一
e. 千葉洋子，沢田宏子
f. ㈱ティー・グラバー
g. 大峡章禧男
h. この施設がサンピエトロ広場を意識しているところから楕円のフォルムにパターン模様を配した。
i. ステンレス
j. ㈱ティー・グラバー

a. KUKI CULTURE CENTER SIGN PLANNING
b. Kuki-shi, Saitama
c. Kuki City
d. Tetsuichi Tomonaga
e. Hiroko Chiba, Hiroko Sawada
f. T. GLOVER Co., Ltd.
g. Akio Ouhazama
h. This circular construction was patterned with the San Pietro square in mind.
i. Stainless steel
j. T. GLOVER Co., Ltd.

a. 戸塚駅前のサイン
b. 神奈川県横浜市
c. 横浜市
d. ㈱GK設計
e. 森田昌嗣，中井川正道
f. ヤマクニ㈱
g. 仲佐写真事務所
h. 戸塚駅東口の三つの駅ビル，広場，ペデストリアン
　デッキ，ストリートファニチュアなどの色調と形態を統
　一してデザインされている。
i. ステンレスパイプ/アルミ板/シルクスクリーン印刷
j. ㈱GK設計

a. SIGN, TOTSUKA STATION
b. Yokohama-shi, Kanagawa
c. Yokohama City
d. Gk Sekkei Associates
e. Yoshitsugu Morita, Masamichi Nakaigawa
f. Yamakuni Co., Ltd.
g. T. Nacása & Partners
h. This sign design is meant to work together with the
　shape and colors of the three buildings, pedestrian
　deck and street furniture found at the station's
　east exit.
i. Stainless steel pipe, aluminum sheet, silkscreen
　printing
j. GK Sekkei Associates

a. 植物園のサイン
b. 茨城県水戸市
c. 水戸市
e. 瀧光男建築設計事務所
f. ㈱タカタ
i. 花崗岩
j. ㈱タカタ

a. SIGN, MITO MUNICIPAL BOTANICAL PARK
b. Mito-shi Ibaraki
c. Mito City
e. Mitsuo Taki Architects & Associates
f. TAKATA Co., Ltd.
i. Granite
j. TAKATA Co., Ltd.

a. サイン
b. 東京都日野市
c. 東京都多摩動物園
e. 原田昭久
f. ㈱サカエ
g. 岡崎一浩
i. ステンレス/合板
j. ㈱サカエ

a. SIGN
b. Hino-shi, Tokyo
c. The Tokyo Tama Zoo
e. Akihisa Harada
f. Sakae Co., Ltd.
g. Kazuhiro Okazaki
i. Stainless, plywood
j. Sakae Co., Ltd.

a. 標識サイン
b. 東京都世田谷区
c. 世田谷区土木部
d. 世田谷区企画部都市デザイン室
e. AUR 建築・都市・研究・コンサルタント，長島孝一，山路清貴，秋元馨
f. 光和工業㈱
g. 橙木健二
h. 歴史と風格のある静かなたたずまいの街世田谷にある「おもいはせの路」の標識サイン
i. 丹銅板/大谷石/スクラッチタイル
j. ㈱ホクストン

a. SIGNPOST
b. Setagaya-ku, Tokyo
c. Setagaya Ward
d. Urban Design Section, Setagaya Ward
e. AUR Architects Office, Koichi Nagashima, Kiyotaka Yamaji, Kaoru Akimoto
f. Kowa Kogyo Co., Ltd.
g. Kenji Toboku
h. The signpost for "Omoihase Path" in stylish, quiet Setagaya.
i. Red copper plate, stone and scratch tile
j. Houkstone Co., Ltd.

a. 川崎市のサイン
b. 神奈川県川崎市
c. 川崎市
d. ㈱GK 設計
e. 森田昌嗣，マーク　ダンカン，中井川正道
f. ㈱スズオカ
g. 仲佐写真事務所
h. サイン表示面は曲面を用い照明点灯時に光が広がるとともに優しいシャープさを盛り込んだ。
i. ステンレス/アルミ板
j. ㈱スズオカ

a. SIGN
b. Kawasaki-shi, Kanagawa
c. Kawasaki City
d. Gk Sekkei Co., Ltd.
e. Yoshitsugu Morita, Dancan Mark, Masamichi Nakaigawa
f. Suzuoka Co., Ltd.
g. T. Nacása & Partners
h. The sign gives off sharp but gentle reflection in oblique illumination.
i. Stainless and aluminum plate
j. Suzuoka Co., Ltd.

a. 案内サイン
b. 東京都内各所
c. 東京都
d. ㈶余暇開発センター
e. 中岡隆史, 佐藤肇
f. ㈱コトブキ
g. 安藤孝
h. 歴史と文化と現在の時の流れのイメージを御影石とステンレスの組合わせで表現した。
i. 自然石/ステンレス/画面はエッチング
j. ㈱コトブキ

a. GUIDE SIGN
b. Tokyo Metoropolis
c. Tokyo Metoropolis
d. Yoka-kaihatsu Center
e. Takashi Nakaoka, Hajime Sato
f. KOTOBUKI Co., Ltd.
g. Takashi Ando
h. An expression of history, culture, and modern times in stainless steel and granite
i. Natural stone, stainless steel, engraving
j. KOTOBUKI Co., Ltd.

a. 陶板サイン
b. 沖縄県沖縄市
c. 沖縄県
e. 川口寿
f. ㈱コトブキ
g. 安藤孝
h. 画面を保護するため陶板のサインとした。潮風，吸水，凍結などに効果がある。
i. コンクリート/白磁板
j. ㈱コトブキ

a. CERAMIC SURFACE SIGN
b. Okinawa-shi, Okinawa
c. Okinawa
e. Hisashi Kawaguchi
f. KOTOBUKI Co., Ltd.
g. Takashi Ando
h. A sign designed to resist salt spray, wind-borne water and freezing temperatures.
i. Concrete and ceramics
j. KOTOBUKI Co., Ltd.

a. 案内サイン
b. 東京都内各所
c. 東京都
d. ㈶余暇開発センター
e. 中岡隆史，佐藤肇
f. ㈱コトブキ
g. 安藤孝
j. ㈱コトブキ

a. GUIDE SIGN
b. Tokyo Metoropolis
c. Tokyo Metoropolis
d. Yoka-kaihatsu Center
e. Takashi Nakaoka, Hajime Sato
f. KOTOBUKI Co., Ltd.
j. KOTOBUKI Co., Ltd.

a. 別荘入口のサイン
b. 長野県茅野市
c. 三井の森
d. エキスプレス広告社
e. ㈱創研 設計部
f. エキスプレス広告社
g. 島田昭治
i. 防腐処理されたダグラスモミ材/彫込み文字
j. ㈱創研

a. VILLA ENTRYWAY SIGN
b. Chino-shi, Nagano
c. Mitsi-no-mori Co., Ltd.
d. Express Kokoku-sha
e. Design Section, SOUKEN Co., Ltd.
f. Express Kokoku-sha
g. Shoji Shimada
i. Treated Douglas fir and engraved letters
j. SOUKEN Co., Ltd.

a. 説明板
b. 千葉県習志野市
c. 公害防止事業団
d. プレック研究所
e. 黛卓郎
g. 佐藤幸雄
i. 屋根は銅板葺き/柱と板は防腐処理したダグラスモ
　ミ材/アルミにシルクスクリーン印刷
j. ㈱創研

a. EXPLANATORY BOARD
b. Narashino-shi, Chiba
c. The Environmental Pollution Service Corporation
d. PREK Institute Co., Ltd.
e. Takuro Mayuzumi
g. Yukio Sato
i. Copper plate roof, treated Douglas fir beams,
　aluminum plate, silkscreen prints
j. SOUKEN Co., Ltd.

a. 農民公園のサイン
b. 東京都足立区
c. 足立区
d. ㈱国際開発コンサルタンツ
e. 間渕義和
g. 島田昭治
i. 柱は防腐処理したダグラスモミ材/板面はレッドウッ
　ド材/文字彫り込み
j. ㈱創研

a. EXPLANATORY BOARD IN AGRICULTURAL
　PARK
b. Adachi-ku, Tokyo
c. Adachi Ward
d. Kokusai-Kaihatsu Consultants
e. Yoshikazu Mabuchi
g. Shoji Simada
i. Pillars of treated Douglas fir, redwood surface,
　etched and colored letters
j. SOUKEN Co., Ltd.

a. 環境サイン
b. 神奈川県厚木市
c. 厚木市
d. スペース・デザインハッピー，石井敏和
e. 石井敏和，和田誠治
f. ㈱ニュー・アイ
g. 和田誠治
i. ヒバ材/鉄骨
j. スペース・デザインハッピー

a. ENVIRONMENT SIGN
b. Atsugi-shi, Kanagawa
c. Atsugi City
d. Space Design Happy, Toshikazu Ishii
e. Toshikazu Ishii, Seiji Wada
f. New Idea Co., Ltd.
g. Seiji Wada
i. Hiba wood and re-rod
j. Space Design Happy Co., Ltd.

a. 森のかけ橋
b. 神奈川県厚木市
c. 神奈川県
d. 佐藤充
e. 村岡賢二
f. ㈱竹中土木
g. ㈱日本軽金属
h. 自然公園を結ぶ橋として素材，形態，と環境との調和に留意してデザインした
i. 花崗岩/高欄はアルミ鋳物
j. ㈱パシフィックコンサルタンツ

a. FOREST HANGING BRIDGE
b. Atsugi-shi, Kanagawa
c. Atsugi City
d. Mitsuru Sato
e. Kenji Muraoka
f. TAKENAKA DOBOKU Co., Ltd.
g. NIHON KEIKINZOKU Co., Ltd.
h. Design to fit in material and construction style in a forest setting.
i. Granite and aluminum casting
j. Pacific Consultants Co, Ltd.

a. 牛巻橋
b. 愛知県名古屋市
c. 名古屋市
d. 名古屋市
f. 矢作建設㈱，渋谷タイル
g. 博英パブリシティ
i. タイル
j. ダントー㈱

a. USHIMAKI-BASHI BRIDGE
b. Nagoya-shi, Aichi
c. Nagoya City
d. Nagoya City
f. Yahagi Kensetsu Co., Ltd., Shibuya Tile Kogyo Co., Ltd.
g. Hakuei Publicity Co., Ltd.
i. Porcelain ungalazed tile
j. DANTO CORPORATION

a. 新芝橋
b. 東京都港区
c. 港区
d. 港区
e. リョーワ工業㈱
f. 日本国土開発㈱
g. 竹林龍三郎
i. 人工御影石
j. リョーワ工業㈱

a. SHINSHIBA BRIDGE
b. Minato-ku, Tokyo
c. Minato Ward
d. Minato Ward
e. RYOWA INDUSTRY Co., Ltd.
f. JDC CORPORATION
g. Ryuzaburo Takebayashi
j. RYOWA Co., Ltd.

a. 隅田公園桜橋
b. 東京都墨田区＋台東区
c. 台東区
e. ㈱横河環境デザイン事務所，構造計画コンサルタント
f. ㈱タカタ
h. 隅田川に架けられた歩道専用の橋．滑りどめと滑らかさを兼ねて SB 仕上げとした
i. 花崗岩
j. ㈱タカタ

a. SUMIDA PARK SAKURA BRIDGE
b. Sumida-ku, Koto-ku, Tokyo
c. Taito Ward
d. YOKOKAWA ENVIRONMENT DESIGN OFFICE, Kozo Keikaku Consultants Co., Ltd.
f. TAKATA Co., Ltd.
h. A pedestrian only bridge bulit over the Sumida river. Non-slip surface and a smooth appearance are the design emphasis.
i. Granite, tile
j. TAKATA Co., Ltd.

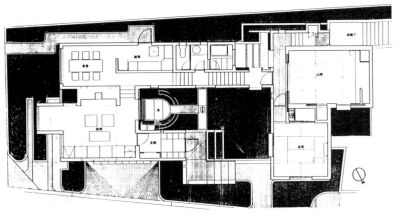

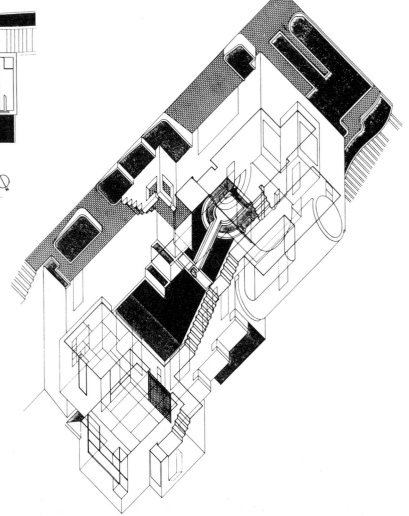

a. 谷崎邸の池
b. 大阪府豊中市
c. 谷崎幸治
d. 出江寛建築事務所
e. 出江寛建築事務所，出江寛，流政之
f. 石井造園
g. スタジオ・村井
h. 小さな中庭が四方から眺められるように設計した。
　 水深3ミリの水が常に滝となって流れ落ちる。
i. 黒御影石/金のオブジェ/玉砂利/ステンレスすの
　 こ/アメリカハナミズキ/さつき
j. 出江寛

a. TANIZAKI RESIDENCE POND
b. Toyonaka-shi, Osaka
c. Koji Tanizaki
d. Kan Izue Architects & Associates
e. Kan Izue Architects & Associates ; Masayuki ;
　 Nagare , Kan Izue
f. Ishii Zoen Co., Ltd.
g. Studio Murai
h. A small garden designed to be viewed from all
　 sides. Water flows and creates a waterfall at three
　 millimeter's depth.
i. Black granite, metal art, sand, stainless steel,
　 cedars and azalea
j. Kan Izue

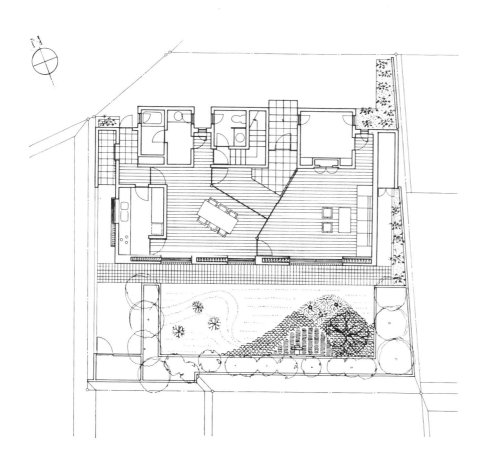

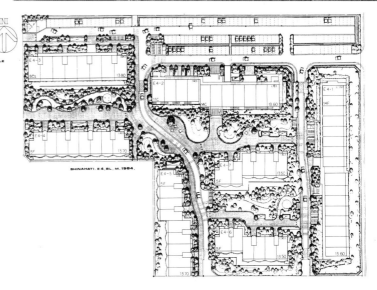

a. 品川区八潮住宅の庭園
b. 東京都品川区
c. 住宅・都市整備公団
d. 藤原清，栗原国男
e. 栗原国男
f. 東光園，生駒造園
g. 栗原国男
h. "ふるさと"になる街づくりをテーマに，石と花をベースとした新しい住宅空間を構成した
i. 花崗岩/エンジュ/ヤマモモ/つつじ/シバザクラ
j. 株あい造園設計事務所

a. PARK TOWN SHINAGAWA YASHIO
b. Shinagawa-ku, Tokyo
c. Housing & Urban Development Corporation
d. Kiyoshi Fujiwara, Kunio Kurihara
e. Kunio Kurihara
f. Toko-en, Ikoma Zoen
g. Kunio Kurihara
h. This housing development design seeks to create the "hometown" feeling with the use of rock and plants in open areas.
i. Granite, interlocking blocks
j. Ai Landscape Planning Co., Ltd.

a. ふれあい花壇
b. 兵庫県神戸市
c. 神戸市
d. 岡田邦彦
e. 藤木寛信，小田信夫
g. 藤木寛信
h. 駅前広場の花壇として誰にも親しめ，人々が出会う
　場所としてデザインした
i. 花崗岩/インターロッキングブロック
j. ㈱アースランドスケープ計画事務所

a. FRIENDSHIP GARDEN
b. Kobe-shi, Hyogo
c. Kobe City
d. Kunio Okada
e. Hironobu Fujiki, Nobuo Oda
g. Hironobu Fujiki
h. A flowerbed garden in the station square, where
　people can feel comfortable and make acquain-
　tances
i. Granite, interlocking brick
j. Earth Landscape Planning Co., Ltd.

a. 雑木林
b. 兵庫県西宮市
c. 雑古昭一
d. 出江寛建築事務所
e. 出江寛建築事務所出江寛
f. 石井造園
g. スタジオ・村井
h. 高い塀を建てないで、傾斜地を利用した雑木林。ポ
　ケット公園として近所の人に解放し親しまれている。
i. 主体となった木はエゴの木（5月に真っ白い花が咲
　く）
j. 出江寛建築事務所

a. ARBORETUM
b. Nishinomiya-shi, Hyogo
c. Shoichi Zakko
d. Kan Izue Architects & Associates
e. Kan Izue
f. Ishii Zoen
g. Studio-Murai
h. This wooded area makes good use of sloped
　ground, without requiring a fence. The neighbor-
　hood will learn enjoy the gentle atmosphere
i. The main growth is egonoki, which flowers in May
j. Kan Izue Architects & Associates

a. 芝生の駐車場
b. 神奈川県横浜市
c. ㈱リコー
d. 清水建設㈱
f. 日本道路㈱
g. ㈱林物産
h. 来客用の芝生駐車場
i. グリーンブロック
j. ㈱林物産

a. TURF PARKING LOT
b. Yokohama-shi, Kanagawa
c. Ricoh Inc.
d. SHIMIZU CORPORATION
f. Nippon Doro Inc.
g. Hayashi Bussan Inc.
h. The grass parking lot contributes a great deal to
　the barren city
i. Green grass
j. Hayashi Bussan Inc.

a. 植物園の階段花壇
b. 茨城県水戸市植物園
c. 水戸市
e. 瀧光男建築設計事務所
f. ㈱タカタ
i. 花崗岩/季節の花
j. ㈱タカタ

a. STEPPED FLOWERBEDS IN A PLANT GAR-
　DEN
b. Mito-shi, Ibaraki
c. Mito City
e. Mitsuo Taki Architects & Associates
f. TAKATA Co., Ltd.
i. Granite, seasonal flowers
j. TAKATA Co., Ltd.

a. 川崎駅の階段花壇
b. 神奈川県川崎市
d. ㈱日建設計
e. ㈱日建設計
g. 仲佐写真事務所
j. ㈱ダイチ

a. FLOWERBED
b. Kawasaki-shi, Kanagawa
d. NIKKEN SEKKEI Ltd.
e. NIKKEN SEKKEI Ltd.
g. T. Nacàsa & Partners
h. This station front flowerbed allows for friendly
　gatherings in the area
j. DAICHI Co., Ltd.

a. ふれあい花壇
b. 兵庫県神戸市
c. 神戸市
d. 岡田邦彦
e. 藤木寛信
g. 藤木寛信,
h. 既存の楠とモニュメントを生かして，ふれあいの場と
　して設計した花壇。
i. 花崗岩/季節の花
j. ㈱アース・ランドスケープ計画事務所

a. FLOWER BED A GATHERING PLACE
b. Kobe-shi, Hyogo
c. Kobe City
d. Kunihiko Okada
e. Hironobu Fujiki
g. Hironobu Fujiki
h. A flowerbed designed around pre-grown camphor
　trees
i. Granite, seasonal flowers
j. Earth Landscape Planning Co., Ltd.

a. 安城駅の花壇
b. 愛知県安城市
d. 環境開発研究所
e. 環境開発研究所
g. 仲佐写真事務所
j. ㈱ダイチ

a. FlOWER BED, ANZYO STATION
b. Anzyo-shi, Aichi
c. Anzyo City
d. ENVIRONMENT DEVELOPEMENT RESEACH INC.
e. ENVIRONMENT DEVELOPEMENT RESEACH INC.
g. T. Nacása & Partners
j. DAICHI Co., Ltd.

a. 新宿公園の公衆便所ほか
b. 東京都新宿区
c. 新宿区土木部公園課
d. ㈱GK設計
e. 森田昌嗣, 中井川正道
f. ㈱スズオカ
g. 野口秀夫
h. 屋根を上空に浮かせ壁を左右にずらし, 自然光を
　取り込む半解放的な空間を作った
i. 耐候性鋼/ステンレス/ラスタータイル/樹脂ガラス
j. ㈱スズオカ

a. SHINZYUKU PARK STREET FURNITURE
b. Shinzyuku-ku, Tokyo
c. Park Section of Civil Engineering, Shinzyuku Ward
d. GK Sekkei Associates
e. Yoshitsugu Morita, Masamichi Nakaigawa
f. Suzuoka Co., Ltd.
g. Hideo Noguchi
h. All around matching furniture
i. Weather resistant stainless steel, tile, laminated glass
j. Suzuoka Co., Ltd.

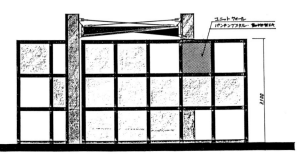

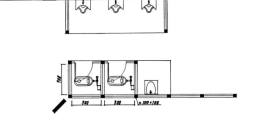

a. 府中公園野外ステージ
b. 東京都府中市
c. 府中市
d. 大間武
e. 大間武
f. 府中植木㈱
g. 大間武
h. 中心市街地につくられた野外ステージ。音楽会、演劇、遊び場など多目的に気軽に利用されている。
i. 円形ステージは擬石大谷石張/観覧席となる階段は稲田石洗いだし仕上げ
j. ㈱住環境設計

a. STAGE IN THE FUCHU PARK
b. Fuchu-shi, Tokyo
c. Fuchu City
d. Takeshi Ohma
e. Takeshi Ohma
f. Fuchu Ueki
g. Takeshi Ohma
h. A facility for the center of the market planned for the various purposes of music, play and children's use
i. The stage design is constructed of imitation Oya stone, the step-seats Inada flagstones
j. Living Environment planers Co., Ltd.

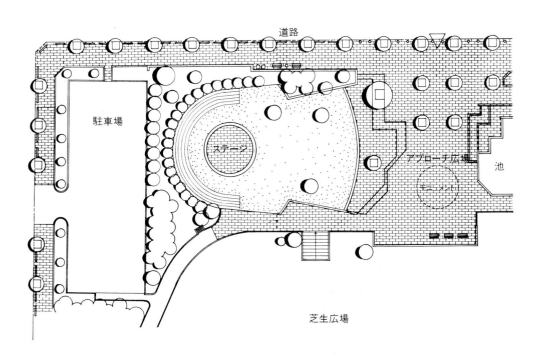

a. 装飾街路灯
b. 東京都新宿区
c. 四谷大通商店街街づくり委員会
d. ホクストン 高司誠
e. ホクストン デザイン オフィス 稲生武彦
f. ㈱浅沼組
g. 橙木健二
h. 迎賓館への歩道を彩る風格と気品を備えた新しいモール街にふさわしいデザインを狙った
i. ダクタイル鋳鉄
j. ㈱ホクストン

a. DECORATIVE LIGHTING
b. Shinzyuku-ku, Tokyo
c. Yotsuya Odori Shopping Street Committee
d. Hawkstone, Makoto Takaji
e. Hawkstone, Design Office, Takehiko Inao
f. Asanuma-Gumi Co., Ltd.
g. Kenji Tohoku
h. An appropiate design for the street leading to the special VIP visitor center
i. Dactile Casting
j. Hawkstone Co., Ltd.

a. Y邸庭園灯
b. 神奈川県藤沢市
c. 吉田邸
d. ㈱創研
e. 伊藤正弘
f. (有) 緑庭園
g. 島田昭治
h. 夜間は低い位置からの照明でソフトな光を放ち、日中は造形物としても落ち着いて鑑賞できるように工夫したデザイン
i. カルフォルニアレッドウッド集成材/白熱灯
j. ㈱創研

a. Y RESIDENCE GARDEN ILLUMINATION
b. Fujisawa-shi, Kanagawa
c. Yoshida
d. SOUKEN Co., Ltd.
e. Masahiro Ito
f. Midori Teien
g. Shoji Shimada
h. Low-hung lights provide soft illumination at night, and blend in well during the daytime
i. California redwood and white lights
j. SOUKEN Co., Ltd.

a. 房総のむら内の照明
b. 千葉県 印旛郡
c. 千葉県教育庁
d. アーバンデザインコンサルタント
e. 大西浩
f. 竹内建設㈱
g. 山田秀男
h. 江戸時代の農村を復元した施設にマッチさせた, 日本の古い明かりを象徴するデザイン。
i. 水銀灯/特殊防腐処理したダグラスモミ集成材
j. ㈱創研

a. LIGHTING POLE IN BOSO-NO-MURA
b. Inba-gun, Chiba
c. Board of Education, Chiba
d. URBAN DESIGN CONSULTANTS Co., Ltd.
e. Hiroshi Ohnishi
f. Takeuchi Kensetsu Co., Ltd.
g. Hideo Yamada
h. Matching with restorations of old farmhouses to symbolize Japanese traditional lighting
i. Douglas fir
j. SOUKEN Co., Ltd.

a. 新浦安駅の照明
b. 千葉県浦安市
c. 浦安市
d. 都市計画研究所, 河合芳樹
e. 八木健一, 小松孝
f. 清水建設㈱
h. ハイマスト灯は高さ21メートル
i. アルミ
j. 八木造景研究所

a. LIGHTING POLE, NEW URAYASU STATION
b. Urayasu-shi, Chiba
c. Urayasu City
d. Yoshiki Kawai, Urbanic Architects Ins.
e. Kenichi Yagi, Takashi Komatsu
f. SIMIZU CORPORATION
h. A hexagonal light with a twenty-meter-high mast
j. YAGI LANDSCAPE DESIGN OFFICE

a. 安城駅の照明灯
b. 愛知県安城市
d. 環境開発研究所
e. 環境開発研究所
g. 仲佐写真事務所
i. ステンレス
j. ダイチ㈱

a. LIGHTING, IN ANZYO STATION
b. Anzyo-shi, Aichi
d. ENVIRONMENT DEVELOPMENT RESEARCH INC.
e. ENVIRONMENT DEVELOPMENT RESERACH INC.
g. T. Nacàsa & Partners
i. Stainless steel
j. DAICHI Co., Ltd.

a. キャンパスの照明
b. 東京都世田谷区
c. 東京農業大学
d. 東京農業大学造園学科
e. 蓑茂寿太郎
f. ㈱西電工
g. 島田昭治
h. アカデミックな学内に落ち着いた雰囲気を醸し出す
ようデザインした
i. 水銀灯/特殊防腐加工したダグラスモミの集成材
j. ㈱創研

a. LIGHTING POLE IN CAMPUS
b. Setagaya-ku, Tokyo
c. Tokyo Agricultural Univ.
d. Department of Landscape Architecture
e. Jutaro Minomo
f. Seidenko Co., Ltd.
g. Shoji Simada
h. Producing a calm atmosphere on the campus
j. SOUKEN Co., Ltd.

a. 八丈島植物園の照明
b. 東京都八丈島町
c. 東京都八丈島支庁
d. プレック研究所
e. 黛卓郎
f. 和光電材㈱
g. 山田秀男
h. 八丈島の塩害に耐え植物園の環境にマッチし, メン
テナンスフリーの条件を考慮してデザインした
i. 水銀灯/カルフォルニア・レッドウッドの集成材
j. ㈱創研

a. LIGHTING FOR HACHIJO BOTANICAL GAR-
DEN
b. Hachijo-zima, Tokyo
c. Hachijo Branch Office, Tokyo
d. PREC Institute Co., Ltd.
e. Takuro Mayuzumi
f. Wako-Denzai Co., Ltd.
g. Hideo Yamada
h. A maintenance-free solution to the salty weather
of the island.
i. Mercury lamps and California redwood
j. SOUKEN Co., Ltd.

a. パークシティ新川崎の立上り
b. 神奈川県川崎市
c. 三井不動産㈱
d. 三井不動産㈱ 中島幹夫
e. 中島幹夫，都田徹，緒方基秀，飯田清二
f. 鹿島建設㈱，三井建設㈱，鹿島道路㈱，東洋造園
g. 都田徹
h. アイデンティティを出すため要所々々に応じて材料，材質，高さなどをさまざまなバリエーションでデザインンした。
i. 御影石／小松石／コンクリート／木曽石
j. 中島幹大

a. RETAINING WALL & CURB STONE
b. kawasaki-shi, Kanagawa
c. Mitsui Real Estate Development
d. Mitsui Real Estate Development, Mikio Nakajima
e. Mikio Nakajima, Tooru Miyakoda, Motohide Ogata, Seiji Iida
f. KAJIMA Corporation Co., Ltd., MITSUI KENSETSU Co., Ltd., KAJIMA ROAD Co., Ltd., TOYO ZOEN Co., Ltd.
g. Tooru Miyakoda
h. In order to bring out a clear identity various materials were builte up in unique ways.
i. Granite, Komatsu stone, concrete, kiso stone
j. Mikio Nakajima

a. 縁石
b. 神奈川県川崎市
c. 三井不動産㈱
d. 三井不動産㈱，中島幹夫
e. 中島幹夫，都田徹，緒方基秀，飯田清二
f. 鹿島建設㈱，三井建設㈱，鹿島道路㈱，
　東洋造園㈱
g. 都田徹
h. 場所に応じて材料，材質に変化を持たせた
i. 御影石/小松石/コンクリート/木曾石
j. 中島幹夫

a. CURB STONE
b. Kawasaki-shi, Kanagawa
c. Mitsui Real Estate Development
d. Mitsui Real Estate Development, Mikio Nakajima
e. Mikio Nakajima, Tooru Miyakoda, Motohide Ogata,
　Seiji Iida
f. KAJIMA Corporation Co.,Ltd., MITSUI KENSETSU
　Co.,Ltd., KAJIMA ROAD Co.,Ltd.,
　TOYO ZOEN Co., Ltd.
g. Tooru Miyakoda
i. Granite, Komatsu stone, concrete, Kiso stone
j. Mikio Nakajima

a. ワシン坂公園のトレリスとパーゴラ
b. 神奈川県横浜市
c. 横浜市
d. 戸田芳樹
e. ㈱戸田芳樹+風景計画, 地福由紀, 奈木政幸, 小峰貴芳
f. ㈱南港植木ガーデン
g. 伊藤直博
i. 木製
j. ㈱戸田芳樹+風景計画

a. WASHINZAKA PARK TRELLIS & PERGOLA
b. Yokohama-shi, Kanagawa
c. Yokohama City
d. Yoshiki Toda
e. Toda Yoshiki & Fukei Keikaku Associates, Yuki Jifuku, Masayuki Nagi
f. Konan Ueki Garden Co., Ltd.
g. Naohiro Ito
i. Wood
j. Toda Yoshiki & Fukei Keikaku Associates

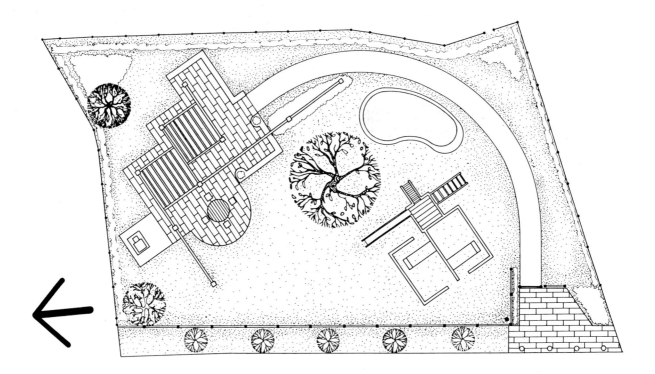

a. 動書による環境デザイン計画
b. 群馬県前橋市
c. 群馬循環器病院
d. 藤波義男
e. 渾彩秀，小堀良夫，小松茂男
f. ㈱小堀石匠苑
g. 岸正一
h. 感情のない打放しのコンクリート壁面に動書で「花」を描き，病院の手厚い看護とうるおいを表現した
i. コンクリート/石彫/ペイント仕上げ
j. ㈱アテンション

a. LANDSCAPE DESIGN BY DYNAMIC CALLIG-RAPHY
b. Maebashi-shi, Gunma
c. Gunma Circulatory Hospital
d. Yoshio Fujinami
e. Saishu Kon, Yoshio Kobori, Shigeo Komatsu
f. Kobori Sekisho-en Co., Ltd.
g. Shoichi Kishi
h. The character "flower" is written over this otherwise blank wall, symbolizing the care and consideration of the hospital
i. Concrete, paint
j. ATENTION Co., Ltd.

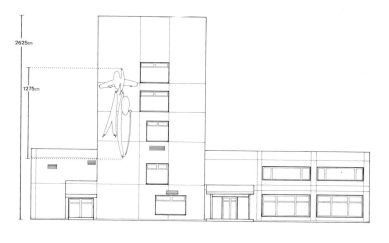

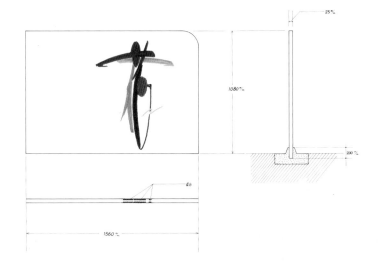

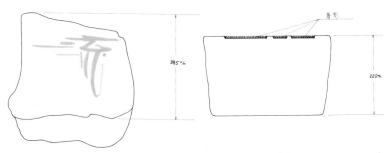

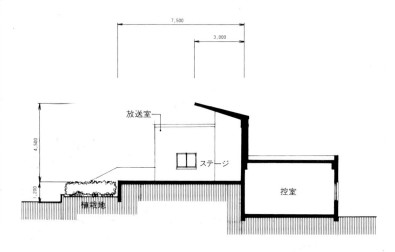

a. 文化の森野外ステージ
b. 東京都瑞穂町
c. 瑞穂町
d. 大間武
e. 塩原孝英、泉田文陽
f. 佐久間建設㈱
g. 大間武
h. 六道山と呼ばれる山の頂上部にある文化の森に建
　設され、祭りやクラブ活動の場として活用されている
i. 反響板は特殊枠を使用/外壁はレンガタイル貼りと
　した
j. ㈱住環境設計

a. STAGE IN THE CULTURAL FOREST
b. Mizuho-machi, Tokyo
c. Mizuho
d. Takeshi Ohma
e. Takahide Shiohara, Fumiaki Izumida
f. Sakuma Kensetsu Co., Ltd.
g. Takeshi Ohma
h. Built on the peak of Rokudo mountain, this facility
　can be used for festivals, and by clubs
i. Special reverberating board on the outer walls
j. Living Environment Planners Co., Ltd.

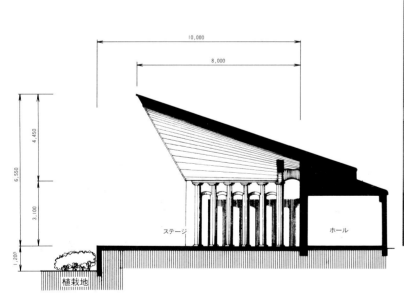

10,000

8,000

6,550
4,450
3,100
1,200

ステージ　　　　　　　　　　　ホール

植栽地

a. 引地台公園野外ステージ
b. 神奈川県大和市
c. 大和市
d. 大間武
e. 塩原孝英
g. 日田篤宏
h. 市制30周年記念事業として市民の文化活動の拠
　点となり，公園のシンボルとなる野外ステージ
i. 壁面は RC づくり/屋根は S づくり/ステージ天井は
　アルミ折板貼とした
j. ㈱住環境設計

a. HIKICHIDAI PARK OUTDOOR STAGE
b. Yamato-shi, Kanagawa
c. Yamato City
d. Takeshi Ohma
e. Takahide Shiohara
g. Atsuhiro Hida (Hida)
h. Thirtieth anniversary of the city's incorporation,
　this stage is a symbol of the park meant as a
　cultural place for the people
j. Living Environment Planners Co., Ltd.

Elements & Total Concept of

URBAN
LANDSCAPE
DESIGN

応募代表者

㈱アース・ランドスケープ計画事務所	〒542 大阪市南区南船場2-7-16 同光ビル6F	☎06-261-8889
㈱あい造園設計事務所	〒156 東京都世田谷区松原2-42-8 吉崎商事ビル	☎03-325-6661
㈱アテンション	〒336 埼玉県浦和市高砂1-13-5	☎0488-22-8956
㈱アルス HED 事業部	〒112 東京都文京区小石川2-21-5	☎03-815-2561
出江寛建築事務所	〒530 大阪市北区南森町1-2-22	☎06-364-3875
㈱稲垣ランドスケープデザイン研究所	〒160 東京都新宿区西新宿3-11-20	☎03-374-7471
㈱INAX	〒104 東京都中央区京橋3-6-18	☎03-561-1710
㈱ウォーターデザイン	〒105 東京都港区新橋6-9-2 新橋第一ビル	☎03-431-8070
内田工業㈱	〒454 愛知県名古屋市中川区好本町3-67	☎052-352-1811
岡本敦生	〒214 川崎市多摩区長沢1-27-7,202	☎044-977-0302
㈱環境美術研究所	〒153 東京都目黒区青葉台2-10-13	☎03-780-3831
㈱空間造形研究所	〒177 東京都練馬区三原台1-23-12	☎03-921-1291
㈱景観設計研究所東京事務所	〒141 東京都品川区東五反田3-18-3	☎03-473-3006
㈱コトブキ	〒100 東京都千代田区有楽町1-2-12	☎03-591-1311
㈱小堀石匠苑	〒370-23 群馬県富岡市黒岩804	☎0274-63-3056
㈱サカエ	〒181 東京都三鷹市新川4-7-19	☎0422-47-5981
サクマ デザインスタジオ	〒154 東京都世田谷区新町1-35-10-402	☎03-426-9915
佐々木著建築設計室	〒730 広島市中区住吉町15-3-802	☎082-249-7633
㈱三英商会	〒270-01 千葉県流山市十太夫108-1	☎0471-53-3141
㈱GK設計	〒171 東京都豊島区南池袋1-11-22	☎03-989-9511
㈱住環境設計	〒151 東京都渋谷区代々木3-24-3	☎03-375-9811
㈱スズオカ	〒144 東京都大田区西六郷3-31-13	☎03-733-5551
スペース・デザイン・ハッピー	〒124 東京都葛飾区新小岩1-37-5	☎03-674-1327
㈱創研	〒167 東京都杉並区荻窪5-10-25 小喜多ビル	☎03-393-5516
綜合デザインセンター	〒464 愛知県名古屋市千種区高見1-26-4 タカミ光ビル	☎052-763-4831
㈱高橋志保彦建築設計事務所	〒105 東京都港区芝1-13-16 芝橋ビル8F	☎03-452-5443
㈱タカタ	〒309 茨城県西茨城郡友部町旭町255	☎02967-7-1173
高橋清	〒194 東京都町田市高坂1598-37	☎0427-25-0576
高野ランドスケープ プランニング㈱	〒164 東京都中野区東中野2-17-23	☎03-365-2711
田辺武	〒754 山口県山口市秋穂二島岩屋	☎0839-84-2230
㈱ダイチ	〒135 東京都江東区東陽3-24-14	☎03-647-1185
第一機材㈱	〒115 東京都北区赤羽1-64-11	☎03-902-9841
ダントー㈱	〒550 大阪市西区江戸堀1-12-8 安田生命ビル	☎06-448-6261
㈱ティー・グラバー	〒141 東京都品川区西五反田3-7-14	☎03-779-6121
㈱東畑建築事務所東京事務所	〒100 東京都千代田区永田町2-4-3 永田町ビル3F	☎03-581-1251
東亜通信工材㈱	〒660 兵庫県尼崎市西長洲本通2-23	☎06-482-0125
㈱東京ランドスケープ研究所	〒150 東京都渋谷区神宮前1-16-4 明東ビル	☎03-404-3601
㈱戸田芳樹＋風景計画	〒160 東京都新宿区新宿5-15-7 東晃ビル9F	☎03-350-8286
凸版印刷㈱	〒110 東京都台東区台東1-5-1	☎03-835-5625
中島幹夫	〒274 千葉県船橋市前原東2-13-14	☎0474-75-5097
㈱長村製作所	〒323 栃木県小山市外城中台90-11	☎0285-24-1251
㈱能登	〒920 石川県金沢市宮保町イ100番地	☎0762-52-1281
㈱林物産	〒150 東京都渋谷区桜丘町12-6 ビラ桜丘3F	☎03-496-6511
速水史朗	〒764 香川県仲多度郡多度津町京盛6-10	☎0877-33-3121
パシフィック コンサルタンツ㈱	〒150 東京都渋谷区神宮前2-8-2	☎03-423-3459
㈱ホクストン	〒112 東京都文京区大塚5-1-17	☎03-943-7511
北海道開発コンサルタント㈱	〒064 北海道札幌市中央区北4条西6丁目 北四条ビル	☎011-231-3760
本間利雄設計事務所＋地域環境計画研究室	〒990 山形県山形市小白川町4-13-12	☎0236-41-7711
丸伊製陶㈱	〒529-18 滋賀県甲賀郡信楽町長野	☎07488-2-0855
㈱八木造形研究所	〒150 東京都渋谷区渋谷3-1-10 タナバビル4F	☎03-486-9620
㈱ヨコタデザインワークスタジオ	〒150 東京都渋谷区猿楽町9-8 代官山パークサイドビレッジ320	☎03-476-5361
横沢彫刻研究所	〒183 東京都府中市本宿町1-32-1	☎0423-66-1167
㈱ランドスケープ デザイン コンサルタント	〒164 東京都中野区東中野1-14-24 吉井ビル	☎03-365-7991
リョーワ工業㈱	〒507 岐阜県多治見市高根町4-21	☎0572-27-6161
㈱脇造園綜合設計	〒870 大分県大分市荷揚町10-13 大分法曹ビル4F	☎0975-34-1436
渡辺隆根	〒171 東京都豊島区長崎6-18-3	☎03-957-2268

索引

撮 影 者

あとがき

　この本に作品の写真とデータを提供していただいた皆様に心からお礼申し上げます。

　また、序文をお寄せくださったガレット・エクボ氏、この企画に対してご助言を賜った中島幹男、都田徹、高野文彰の各氏に深く感謝いたします。

　第1章はランドスケープ・デザインのコンセプトとエレメントの関係を扱い、「全体」を構成している個々のデザイン・エレメントにはどんなものがあるか、ランドスケープの中でどのように生かされているか、どんな役割を果たしているかなどに焦点をあててみました。第2章はデザインのエレメントをいくつかのグループに分類し「個」としての存在を追求しています。

　最近のランドスケープ・デザインの世界的な傾向は、人間も自然の一員であり人間そのものが風景であるとする考えが圧倒的で、ランドスケープ・アーキテクチャーもデザイン技術の優劣を競うだけでなく、多重な社会の構造の中でいかに人間と風景の調和を保っていくかに力点をおいてデザインするようになっています。

　取材中にお目にかかったN氏には教えられることが多く、ランドスケープ・デザインを志すにいたった心境などもお聞きできました。

　山深い鄙びた里で、父は林業を営んでいました。父につれられ植樹にいくのが楽しみでした。苗木と弁当を背負い道なき山道を踏み分けて木を植えたものです。雑木林を切り開いた斜面に穴を掘り、土と落葉をかぶせ近くの谷川から水を汲んできて根元にかけ踏み締めました。父は黙々と苗木を植え、昼飯どきにたった今植えた苗木が風雪に耐え、歳月を経ていかにして一本の樹木に育つかを、朴訥な言葉で語ってくれました。幼少の頃のこうした体験と父の言葉は鮮明に脳裏に焼きつけられおり、今でもデザインの現場で生かされています……と。

　植樹ははじまりであって終わりではない。ランドスケープ・デザインも竣工した瞬間が終わりではなく、はじまりであり、出来上がってから3年5年10年と経過してはじめてその真価が分かってくる。それは樹木を育てることと同じで根気がいる仕事です。

　あらゆるデザインの分野で個と全体との調和が大きなテーマとしていつの世にも問われ続けています。

　ランドスケープ・デザインの場合の個と全体とは、コンセプトとエレメント、クライアントの理解、質の高い施工技術、テーマに適したストリート・ファニチュアの開発、メンテナンス、芸術性に加えて時代性などあらゆる分野からのノウハウを取り入れたり新技術を開発したり、デザインそのものが世の中に受け入れられていくためにぜひともクリアしておかねばならないいくつかの課題があります。

　とくに忘れてならないのは、ランドスケープ・デザインの中にデザイナーが人間として所有しているヒューマンウェア、マインドウェアがその時代を生きる人々にいかに伝わり、感動と喜びを与えていけるかにあるのではないでしょうか。

　この本はそういう意味でそれらの課題を完全に消化しているとはいいがたく、未完です。今後さらに構想をすすめて国際的に通用する視野と規模のヒューマン・ランドスケープ・デザインの書を続刊していくつもりです。皆様の忌憚のないご感想と叱咤、そして今後このシリーズに対するご協力をお願いいたします。

（企画・編集代表　K．T）

Postscript

I would like to sincerely thank all those who contributed materials, pictures and information to this book. I likewise extend my deepest thanks to Mr. Garret Eckbo for composing the introduction, and to Mr. Mikio Nakajima, Mr. Tooru Miyakoda and Mr. Fumiaki Takano, for their invaluable advice and assistance in planning this project.

Chapter One carries example relating to the concept of landscape design in 'total' form. Thus individual design projects are studied to see just what elements are being used, and how these elements function within the landscape. Here the focus is on the role of individual elements. Chapter Two divides the design elements into several categories and studies their 'individual' characters.

Throughout the world the recent trend in landscape design is overwhelmingly toward recognition and treatment of people as natural objects, and thus as elements which must be integrated into the architecture and design, rather than outside elements which technique must-for better or worse-attempt to accomadate.

While collecting materials for this project I was fortunate to learn a great deal about landscape design from Mr. N. In fact I came to understand why this man chose landscape design as his endeavour, and what it truly means to him.

"My father owned and cared for a forest near a small town in the mountains, and I frequently followed him into the woods to plant trees." He says. "We walked along the natural paths of the forest, planting seedlings along the way. We dug holes on deforested slopes, planting with sod and dead leaves, then carried water up from the valley stream, finally watering and tamping the earth under our boots. My father worked without speaking any words, but afterword, as we ate our lunch, he talked in simple words about the life of the seedling, the snowstorms it would endure as it grew through each year. The images and words of this time left an indelible mark in the boy's memory, and as a man these ideas influence the designs I create."

The planting of a tree marks a beginning, not an end. Likewise, a design is not finished with the planning or construction, but rather only just begun. It is after three or five or ten years that the value of any design can be appreciated-just as it is with the growth of a tree.

The question of individual design, within the total environment, will continue to be a major theme in all areas of design. In landscape design the elements, as they stand within the whole, must be applied with the full understanding of the client, with the highest quality materials, and the know-how of modern science and art. The development of appropriate street furniture and good maintenance are also points of great inportance if landscape design is to be appreciated throughout the world. These are all points which must be made clear themes in landscape design.

Certainly one point which must not be forgotten in landscape design is the designer's own body and human mind, so that people can feel and enjoy and understand what the designer has created.

Unfotunately this book probably does not fully satisfy all the themes and questions it addresses. Hopefully we can follow up this volume with another international view on the subject of Human Landscape Design. Any thoughts or criticisms you might offer would be greatly appreciated.

(Chief editor, K.T.)

トータル・ランドスケープ・エレメント

Elements & Total Concept of URBAN LANDSCAPE DESIGN

発行／1988年4月25日初版第1刷発行

編集／グラフィック社編集部

編集協力／中島幹夫、都田徹、高野文彰

翻訳／スコット ブラウス (Scott Brause)、都田徹

装丁／清野尹良

本文レイアウト／清野尹良

発行者／久世利郎

印刷・製本／錦明印刷株式会社

写植／三和写真工芸株式会社

発行所／株式会社グラフィック社

　　　　〒102 東京都千代田区九段北1－9－12

　　　　Tel. 03-263-4318 振替・東京3－114345

定価／12,000円

ISBN4-7661-0475-7 C3070 ¥12000